New Hampshire's Emerging Writers
Writers
An Anthology

Compiled and Edited by
Z Publishing House

2018

D1509135

Table of Contents

Foreword, or How This Series Came to Be 5

Prodigal Son (Reggie Bourn) 7

The Secret Admirers (Theresa Suarez) 10

Dear Husband (Devin R. Wilkie) 15

The Sands of Time (Niquie J) 18

Lori and Mr. Deer (Jenell M. Boyd) 23

Underground (James L. Kaiser) 27

The Simplicity of Dried Apricots (G.R. Weslo) 29

The Execution of Fredrick Harper McElhenny (Jayson Robert Ducharme) .. 37

How to Ruin Steak (Casey Kimball-Marfongelli) 41

A Piece of Us (Lauren Ashley) 45

Shattered (Kate Johnston) 50

Dead Reckoning (Leo T.F. Martin) 59

Just Off Main Street (Kari Nguyen) 63

Parenthood (Marina White) 68

Recognition (Scott M. Baker) 70

St. Germaine and Blinking Colored Lights (Kelly Dalke) 75

Blue-Collar Father (Nolan R. O'Connell) 84

11.2.16 (Stacy Hannings) 88

Fields of Forgotten Lessons (Elizabeth R. Jurgilewicz) 91

How Horses Heal (Carter Saltmarsh) 93

The Last Lap (Stephanie Martin Glennon) 97

Benedictine and Me (Nicole Turner) 103

Note to the Reader 111

About Z Publishing House 113

Author Biographies 115

Foreword, or How This Series Came to Be

There is a troubling catch-22 that exists in the world of publishing: in order to be published—at least by any of the major houses—you must already have been published. The logic works like this: Publishing houses want to sell books. What easier way to sell books than by publishing authors who already have amassed large followings of readers to whom they can market? Inevitably, this cycle leaves the aspiring author with the pressing question of where to begin. Sure, the dramatic rise of self-publishing platforms has enabled everyone to put their writing out there, which is great, but it does come with its own set of problems. Namely, when everyone actually does put their writing out there, as has happened, the question now becomes: Where are the *readers* to begin? With the oversaturation of the market, readers could spend entire lifetimes buying and reading self-published books and still not find that one author with whom they truly resonate. On Amazon alone, for instance, a new book is uploaded every five minutes, and that number is only set to rise as more and more people take advantage of the self-empowering platforms available to writers today.

The good news is that readers want to discover new talent. This we learned firsthand after beginning Z Publishing in November of 2015. What started as a small Facebook group designed to bring independent writers together on a shared platform of exposure soon transcended into a wave of newfound appreciation for independent writing. Within a few short months, Z Publishing had amassed tens of thousands of followers across social media. Once we knew the idea had struck a chord with a growing group of people, we took the next step and launched Z Publishing's own website in March of 2016. Publishing articles from writers of a multitude of genres—including travel, fiction, politics, lifestyle, and poetry—the website garnered more support from readers and writers alike, and our following continued to grow.

Furthering upon our mission to promote the work of talented wordsmiths across the nation, we began a series called America's Best Emerging Poets, through which we showcased our favorite up-and-coming poets on a state-by-state basis. After the success of our first series, we decided to open submissions to prose writers as well. Thus began our Emerging Writers series, a collection of short writings from a wide variety of genres—including literary fiction, mystery, and narrative nonfiction—through which we hope to offer our readers a quick and efficient way to discover new local talent and perhaps entirely new genres that otherwise may have been too daunting to explore.

While working on this series, and as our base of physical retailers has expanded, we've also been able to take perhaps the most significant step forward in our publishing evolution, and we now proudly offer solo-author book deals. To make the selections on who to offer these deals to, we will take into account reader reviews, so if there are any writings within this book that you particularly enjoy, be sure to give them a mention in your Amazon review!

Now that you know a bit about how this series came to be, we'd like to thank you for taking the time to explore this edition of the Emerging Writers series. We hope you enjoy this publication, and we look forward to hearing your thoughts regarding how, together, we can build the publishing house of the future.

-The Z Publishing Team

Prodigal Son
Reggie Bourn

The moment he stepped out of the car, Andrew felt his footsteps becoming heavy. He'd made up his mind on the drive over but as soon as he caught sight of the house, his enthusiasm evaporated like steam. Andrew's gaze drifted down from the roof towards the door, and he forced himself to take another step. The old house was a little rough around the edges, with peeling paint and dusty windows, but it held a prominent place in the young man's heart.

It was home.

Home in the past tense, Andrew reminded himself. He hadn't set foot on the lawn since he was seventeen, an age that felt like a lifetime ago. He had left boasting of his imminent wealth, the riches that never came, that had never existed. When his family tried to help him, Andrew had pushed them away, exiling himself from his home. These circumstances had created a crippling fear of coming home, and the resulting fear of how his family would react.

He took another step, his boot crushing a pile of dry leaves underfoot.

Andrew stole another glance at the house and found memories flooding back, both good and bad. There was the flower garden which his mother had always fussed over the amount of rocks in the soil. Next to the porch sat a short statue of a laughing cherub, its metal features stained with a greenish-blue patina.

Andrew stepped past the stump of the oak tree that had been in the front lawn for as long as he had lived. He could remember the day when he had carved his initials next to Emmy's, scratched into the flesh of the tree as one final memento of their relationship. They'd fallen in love over their desire for money, and when Emmy told him about the gold vein she'd heard rumors about, he leaped at the chance.

Like the tree, she was gone now. She'd never turned back on the chance to be rich and in doing so, abandoned Andrew when he doubted her claims. Everyone had abandoned him, their relationships shallow and worthless as the dirt beneath his feet.

Andrew shook his head to send the memories away and found himself standing in front of the front door. It had taken only a few minutes to walk to the stoop, but to Andrew they felt like hours. He stared at the painted blue door and searched his soul for the strength to knock.

Andrew raised a shaking fist and rapped on the wooden door. The silence that followed was all the time his mind needed to conjure up the infinite number of outcomes for the situation. Would his parents answer or not show up at all? Did they even want to see him again, after how he'd left, cursing their names?

Andrew jumped back to reality at the sound of the door opening and stared into the eyes of his father. Like the house, his face showed the signs of aging and his hair was much whiter than it had been three years ago.

"Hello, Andrew."

His father's words were like a bullet, striking the fear in his heart. Andrew took a deep breath and found the words he had been looking for.

"Hey, Dad. Look, I'm sorry—"

Whatever he would say next was cut off by his father's warm embrace. Andrew froze for a moment, then returned the gesture. Once they separated, he wiped his eyes and smiled, an expression he hadn't felt in a while.

"Dad, I know you're probably wondering why I'm back, but all I want you to know is that I want to come home. I'm sorry for what happened before, with Emmy." Andrew explained, finding confidence with each word. His father smiled at him.

"I'm glad you've come home. Come inside, your mother won't believe me unless you tell her yourself."

Andrew nodded his head and followed his father back inside the house. They approached the living room and he heard the chatter of the television playing.

"Who was that?" his mother called out.

"See for yourself." Andrew's father replied, and they stepped into the room.

When she caught a glimpse of him, Andrew's mother's eyes widened and she bolted up from her chair. Andrew opened his mouth to speak and found himself swept into a crushing hug.

He was home.

The Secret Admirers
Theresa Suarez

Two hours, forty-nine minutes, and seven seconds. That was all the time Jack had until the 5 p.m. New York-bound bus rolled out of Boston and the love of his life would disappear from his sight forever. Jack was only twenty-two but old enough to take life seriously. If she was gone, so would his dreams of a beautiful life together. If she was gone, nothing would matter anymore and the sky would always seem black, unlike today's sun reflecting off the snow and pouring in from the old library's window. Besides his own dreams—hadn't he ruined Lilly's?

As Jack was letting these thoughts unthaw, he sunk into the nearest chair and felt as if he would keep sinking. Hot tears leaked from the rough worker's hands that covered his face. Every second, the grandfather clock across the expansive room reminded him that time was running out.

The canary, as nondescript as ever, sat in her too-fancy cage, tilting her yellow head to the side. She chirped out of time with the clock.

Jack squeezed his right hand into a fist as if crushing those letters. *Five* of them in the past two-and-a-half years he and Lilly had been dating. Each one had contained a different problem or dream for which she had asked her old friend *Rob's* advice, but each one was ultimately the same: addressed not *Dear Jack* but *Dear Rob*. When Jack finally opened his squinted-shut eyes, he saw that the canary's pretentiously decorated cage door could easily creak open with a gentle flick of the handle.

"Sorry, I'm a little late." Jack's granddad stood in the doorway of the old mansion's library. He was even more impressive than the hundreds of treasure-worthy books stacking up to the neck-craning ceiling, like bricks made of the greatest literature. Maybe it was because Granddad was made of the greatest virtues, Jack decided. From one look at the man, Jack thought, one could see that his eyes shone with both a brilliance that defied his many decades and a tender-heartedness that had never failed him.

"You wanted to see me about Lilly. How is she?"

Jack sighed either out of relief or distress. "She's good. Actually not really. She seemed stressed a week ago, the last time I talked to her. She's about to get on a bus and, well, live her life without me because well, I like kind of messed things up—but it's not that I don't want her to be happy. I just . . ." As if cutting off his own sentence, Jack's hand automatically felt the tiny box in his large jeans pocket, a box he hadn't taken long to get accustomed to feeling. This time Granddad didn't ask his grandson which book he wanted to read together today.

"What are you holding in your fist?" The old man asked.

"Nothing," Jack said plainly, wondering what the old man meant.

"Are you sure?"

The young man looked at the canary's wings. "Yea, nothing."

As an exception to her own rule, Lilly felt her posture slipping away from Straight as she looked at herself one last time in the office's restroom mirror. Okay, *this* would be the last time. Somehow it was the only way to find out who she was when she felt like a stranger to herself. In fact, even when she saw the same brown freckles, pale skin, red hair, and determined, bright eyes she had always seen for twenty-two years, it was an entirely unfamiliar person looking back at her today. A hand went up to trace the shape of her cheek, a cheek that someone else had known for a long time. Two-and-a-half years was a long time. She wasn't necessarily breaking things off—for good—no, how could I live with that, she thought. She was breaking free of this old life in this city and having to deal with unbreakable silences on the phone that were the reason why she wrote those letters. Sometimes her tongue would feel tied, and she didn't know why. Why were her problems so hard to talk about? She finger-combed her hair and clutched it, frustrated with herself.

Lilly tied her hair into a ballet bun without looking in the mirror. New York was only . . . how long away? The young woman checked her work watch for the hundredth time. Three fifty-three. Fists through coat sleeves, scarf wrapped tightly but not choking, tucking pants into salt-encrusted boots, hands slipped through gloves, and pulling over a hat. Saying goodbye and "Happy Valentine's Day!" to each co-worker with a string of prepared phrases and one practiced smile. Heavy staccato notes down the cold stairs. Out the doors and into a gust of wind. Her letter! Lilly snatched it out of the air before it could be swirled around Boston, lost forever.

The grandfather clock struck four. As if springing him into action, at the first chime Jack leaped from his chair. Mumbling a thank you to Granddad, pounding across the wood floor and leaving streaks of melted snow, Jack threw open the thick, oak front door and slipped on the ice. *Nothing that will hurt me*, he thought. Standing back up, in one motion he bounced into the company truck and turned the key. One, two, ten tries of starting the truck, and many more tries of jump-starting it, but just spinning wheels . . .

While Jack dialed a couple of numbers on his phone, back inside the library the canary stared into the world as if for the first time. "Little bird," Granddad whispered, "Your door is open."

Normally she would have counted the number of Patriots

hats in bustling South Station as she and Jack waited for the bus, but today all she could count was the number of happy couples and the minutes between now and five p.m. It was a wild, crazy thought, and probably not responsible, but Lilly did the math: twenty to thirty minutes was all it would take to deliver the letter to Jack and come back in time for the bus, and maybe she would know what to say, and explain how she had been totally wrong, and he would apologize, and maybe after talking out a plan, their future wouldn't have to be separate after all.

"Hey, watch it!"

"Sorry!"

Lilly watched from across the room as a young man butted through the crowd, sending too-long coat sleeves and wayward scarves flapping amid a flock of disgruntled people. A smile snuck into Lilly's lips. That could only be Jack. Was it true after all? That couldn't be Jack, because if he would have come, this is exactly how she had just been picturing it.

As Jack finished panting, he scanned the crowd and found Lilly now standing at her favorite table, by the ever-changing row of vender's kiosks. Without thinking, the two lovers took a few steps toward each other until they stood close enough to hug. And that's exactly what they did. After a long time, in which they neither counted nor needed to count the seconds, Lilly pulled out an envelope from her pocket. It was sealed in old-fashioned-looking red wax in the shape of a heart and addressed *"To Jack. Love, Lilly."* But Jack didn't even have to open the letter to know what it said, because a face tells more than a thousand words, and Lilly couldn't help smiling with a glow that repeated, *"You came."* In turn, he pulled out a paper lunch bag from his coat pocket and handed it to her. "For the road," he offered shyly.

"I'm sorry for not being someone you could talk to about your dreams or your problems," Jack said. "I get why you

13

felt like Rob was the only one—"

Lilly stopped him with a kiss.

"I thought you would be mad I was here," Jack confessed.

"Oh, no! I was actually hoping you'd come. Read the letter," Lilly insisted, still smiling. Then her smile faded as she looked down at the ground. "I just thought you would have never been open to me pursuing this dance opportunity. I'm so sorry I shut you out . . . You've always been my number one supporter . . . I should have known you would have listened if only I'd—"

Jack hugged her tighter. "It's okay, I forgive you! You're fine," he said warmly. "Do you forgive me?"

"Of course, love," Lilly couldn't pour the words out quickly enough.

Jack asked, "One more question?"

Dear Husband

A Response to Egon Hostovsky's "The Hideout"
Devin R. Wilkie

You're gone. You're gone and I can't understand why.

Initially, I believed you when you told me you were only going to Ostrava; you would be back in a few days. It was a business trip, you assured me; the girls and I would be fine. You left in the night to make better time.

That was four years ago.

At first, I worried that director of yours was behind it somehow. Schwartz had wanted those blueprints of yours so badly; when you told him you burned them, his ire permeated the silence of the room. He told you to redraw them; when you refused and he pressed harder, I wanted to speak up, but I knew you would be held responsible. He had already been lost to the Germans, and nothing we could do would suffice for him. So I kept my quiet and let his tirade continue. Oh, did he try to report you? I worried that he might. If someone should wonder whether the blueprints still existed, or whether you might be able to reproduce them . . . I don't know what I'm saying. In any case, you need not worry long: there are whispers that the war will be over soon.

I hope you will return to us before long. Johanna and Marta have grown so much. They are twenty and twenty-two now; I hope that I have been a good mother to them these past years. Marta has been married a year now; her husband is not wealthy, but he treats her well and they do not want for food. Hanna met a man a few weeks ago and has not ceased talking about him since. He is a lawyer, she raves. Not like Marta's violinist. A man of the world—well-traveled, highly educated, he studied in Germany—

The Germans are still here; since they moved in, they have

become a fixture of the country. They are on our trains; they are in our markets. One of the soldiers comes to visit us regularly; I am certain he is checking to see if we have heard from you. Alas, we have heard nothing from you, and the house never changes, so he always leaves quickly. To be honest, I wish it were different. I wish we had a letter from you to hide, or a gift from wherever you have been living since we last saw you, or something else to draw the curiosity of the soldier. Something new, that is, something foreign, that will cause him to ask me where I found it, for me to hurriedly invent an excuse, that I am redecorating or that I received it from an uncle in Paris or that it has always been here, but in a different room.

Why did you refuse Director Schwartz? He did not want much from you. The blueprints would have been easy for you to redraw, and the Germans would have built the gunsight absent further input from you. Perhaps the French would even find the blueprints, and you would not have been responsible for influencing the outcome of the war. Perhaps they are developing similar technology. Perhaps . . .

Oh, I hope you did not offer your blueprints to the French. The Germans would not allow you to return home after such a slight, and they may even punish your family for your transgression.

I still have hope, my love. If your blueprints were found, aircraft would not be able to fly over the enemy without fear of being shot down. They still fly freely and then return, and so I hold out hope that you have not been taken and that you have not betrayed the men who hold your family and your country hostage.

But then, where are you? Have you hidden yourself in Czechoslovakia, somewhere among us, where the soldiers do not recognize you? Have you perhaps fled to France, hiding out among the people who would protect you from the

Germans? But no; explain to them your reasons for hiding, and they will want from you the very thing you do not wish to give. They are not bad people, but this is war. You would need to hide behind anonymity; you are not a political man, my love, and I know you could keep your opinions subdued. And that is why I hold out hope that you are alive and well.

Perhaps you have hidden with Madame Olga in France. She fancied you, I know, and she would have been willing to hide you. Perhaps she would want your affections in return, but I know you would not betray me.

I heard stories of a Czechoslovak man who died provoking the conflict earlier this year. A freight ship carrying German weapons was sunk from within; it appears the man was intentionally trying to open the ship using its own inner workings. The men who escaped safely said the man drowned in his pursuit, but that he had accomplished what he had intended before the water rushed in and took him. Oh, how our friends tried to shield me from the story! The man was an engineer, and so they guessed that it may have been you, but I do not believe them, for you are still alive, my love! You are in hiding, and when the war is over and the Germans have left Czechoslovakia you will return to me and we will be together again for the remainder of our lives. We will host a grand ball upon your return, and we shall invite all our friends and neighbors to come and celebrate the end of the war, but we shall be celebrating your safe return!

Alas, my hope wanes, but I cannot allow it to die, not yet. I cannot extinguish the flame of hope, no matter how faint it burns this day, four years exactly since you left. I intend to see you when this war is over, and so I will not allow myself to consider that this will not happen. Until then, my love, I wait for you.

The Sands of Time
Niquie J

The sands of Egypt rippled. Houses trembled as the land shook dangerously. Outside, cries of panic erupted as people ran for cover. Dogs howled and cattle brayed. Inside the grandiose walls of the royal palace, the chaos was no different. Servants ducked inside doorways, abandoning their duties in a bid for safety. Inside the great hall, gasps of surprise were uttered from the gathered courtiers, as those standing fought to remain upright. The walls themselves seemed to groan, as dozens of frightened gazes darted around the chamber.

Then, as suddenly as it began, it was over.

Over the soft murmurs of bewildered queries, one voice rang out loud and clear. "Is everyone alright?"

Standing from his gilded throne, the young Pharaoh Kheti surveilled the audience chamber. Members of the court were helping others who had fallen back to their feet, while shaken servants began to clean up the mess. While the quake had been nerve-wracking, it did not appear to have been damaging.

"I believe that everyone is fine, my lord," Merisu, the sagely vizier answered, stepping away from the pillar that he had used to maintain his balance.

Kheti gave the room another cursory look, before accepting his adviser's words and reclaiming his seat. He then ran a quivering hand across his forehead. "Anen, take your men into the city. Aid anyone in need."

The Commander nodded, then motioned for several nearby soldiers to follow him. As they left, Kheti turned to the Captain of the Palace Guard. "Nuya, have your guards spread out across the palace, see if anyone was injured."

"Yes, Pharaoh."

Kheti watched as the men set out, before returning his attention to the rising cacophony around him. "Merisu, let us try and restore some order here, shall we?"

Consciousness returned to Leah with all the delicacy of an elephant. For several minutes, she remained perfectly still on the hard surface upon which she laid, the simple act of breathing seemed to send knives bouncing around her skull. With a soft moan, Leah gingerly opened her eyes.

She was face down on a stone floor, it appeared. A dusty floor. The grit was everywhere, tickling her nose. Looking past that, she took in her surroundings. The room she was in was large, and quite ornately decorated. A grand four-poster bed sat along the far wall, along with several chests and some furniture. The walls were covered in the same glyphs that she had been staring at back in the museum, as alien to her as algebra. And the gold! She had never seen so much gold in her life. The room was covered in it—the bed, furniture, even the walls. She appeared to be in some very ritzy bedroom.

Exhaling, Leah closed her eyes. Great; she had a relative idea of where she was, now she just had to figure out where *here* is.

The sudden sound of pounding feet alerted Leah to the fact that she was no longer alone. However, before she could decide whether to get up and hide, she felt strong, calloused hands wrap around her arms, quickly hauling her to her feet. Her world tilted sickeningly at the abrupt change, threatening to reintroduce her lunch. The hands on her arms tightened painfully in response to her swaying.

"Who are you?"

Even through the roaring in her ears, Leah could hear the

stern authority in the tone of the speaker. It wasn't the kind of authority that you developed overnight. Unable to resist, she opened her eyes, forcing them to focus on the face that was almost directly in front of hers.

He seemed to be a middle-aged man, but well-built. His face was slightly weathered, with dark eyes emboldened by a black liner. He was clothed only in sandals and some type of loincloth, though he had a wicked looking weapon sheathed at his hip.

"I ask again: who are you."

Jolted from her jumbled thoughts, Leah tried to focus. "Leah."

"How did you get inside the palace?"

That threw her. "Palace?"

"Yes. How did you get into the palace?"

Leah honestly had no answer to that. "I . . . I don't know."

The man before her grunted. Then one of the men holding her up straightened. "What shall we do with her, sir?"

The first man—who seemed to be in charge—considered her for a moment. It was hard not to squirm under the intense gaze. "We'll take her before the Pharaoh. He can then pass judgment."

Leah was sure nothing else in that moment could've spun her head as much as those words had. "Wait a minute. Wait. Did you say *pharaoh*?"

The men ignored her and proceeded to drag her from the room. As she was led out into a large corridor, Leah couldn't help but wonder if this was all just some figment of her concussed mind.

Kheti was just signing off on the last list of damages when the throne room doors opened, emitting Nuya and his troop. While that in and of itself wasn't anything of particular note—it would not have taken long to secure the palace—what was surprising was the petite figure hanging between two of the guards.

"My lord, we found this intruder in the Royal Bedchambers," Nuya announced without preamble.

The young king raised an eyebrow. "*My* bedchambers?" He peered at the prisoner, a young woman, it seemed, and an exotic-looking one at that. But he was certain that he had never seen her before. "And just what was this intruder doing in my chambers?"

"Nothing, your Highness. She was on the floor. She appeared unconscious."

Kheti nodded. "So no evidence of malicious intent or thievery?"

"No, my king."

The pharaoh rose from his throne, descending the steps towards the prisoner. "Did she tell you anything?"

"Nothing."

Striding over to the young woman, Kheti motioned for the guards to release her. "I am Pharaoh Sekhemre Kheti. Perhaps you will tell me your name?"

Leah, having quietly listened to the entire conversation, suddenly realized that *she* was being addressed. By the *pharaoh*. How was this even possible? Fifteen minutes ago she was on a field trip at the local museum and now she was in ancient Egypt? Surely she must be suffering from a bad concussion—or brain damage, even. There was no way any of this could be real. However, the weapons carried by the men around her *looked* pretty real, so it probably wouldn't hurt to play along.

Lifting her head and steeling her nerves, Leah looked up at the man before her.

He was nothing like she expected. Youthful and athletic, he appeared only a few years older than herself. He was wearing similar garments as the men around them, though the golden jewelry adorning his person were a dead giveaway of his regal status. Dark swirls of hair stuck out from beneath the crown atop his head, while eyes the color of desert sand held her own with curious patience. He was actually rather attractive, speaking purely from an objective point of view.

Remembering that she had an audience undoubtedly awaiting her answer to their king, Leah cleared her throat, forcing the fog from her mind and straightening her posture. The last thing that she wanted to do was let these men think that she was some demure creature they could bend to their will. When she was finally composed, she met the king's gaze.

"My name is Leah Kingston. And you won't believe where I'm from."

Lori and Mr. Deer
Jenell M. Boyd

It's summer vacation, and I'm eleven years old. I live in a two-bedroom apartment on the top floor of a house with my older brother, Eddie, instead of living with our mom. Eddie owns a restaurant our dad bought back in the 1970s. Dad died in 1982, just before I turned three. His name was Ed, and he liked baseball and had blue eyes. I don't remember him, but when I see pictures of him, I feel happy. He looked like a nice person.

Eddie works during the week, and I'm usually with a babysitter, which is okay, but I am getting older. Today, he left me with Mr. Deer, who lives on the first floor. He's over six feet tall and wears jeans from head to toe, and sometimes he smells a little smoky from cigarettes. Mr. Deer keeps an old tomahawk and a peace pipe in his living room, and he tells me about his grandfather, who used to be a medicine man.

Today, Mr. Deer had to get something from his doctor, and they're over in Lancaster. That's where he used to live before moving to Harrisburg last year. It's a long drive, and his pickup truck feels bumpy. The radio doesn't work at all, so he asks me how my summer is going. I told him how Eddie and I went to our Cousin Roy's wedding in Baltimore. Roy is very whiney, and married a boring woman named Polly, and she has a handsome twin brother. His name is Louis, and he took me dancing.

The doctor's office is boring. The music playing on the speakers is bad, and I wish I had a lollipop, but the women at the desk said they don't have any. She has Farrah Fawcett hair, except it's brown instead of blonde. My sister Alice tried doing that to her hair once, and she burned herself instead. After we leave the doctor's office, Mr. Deer takes me to a coffee shop. The waitress calls us both 'Hon'. I get a sticky bun and a glass of milk. Mr. Deer drinks black coffee and a couple of plain cake donuts, which he likes to dip into the coffee.

We took the backroads back to Harrisburg because Mr. Deer said it's more scenic. We're halfway home when we see a horse-drawn buggy on the side of the road. I think it would be neat if we traveled by horses still, and I ask Mr. Deer if he likes horses. He starts to say he does, then both of his eyes get real big, like bug out of their sockets big.

"Looks like that buggy had a major malfunction," he said, and I looked back out the window. The horse stopped working.

Its legs crumpled, and it fell forward, face first, into a coffee colored puddle. The buggy jerked and tilted to the side, and the guy inside jumped out before it tipped over completely. He looked Amish. They live all over Pennsylvania, and we learned about them in school. Mr. Deer stopped the truck beside the man and asked if he needed a ride.

"Sure!" The man laughs. I don't know why he's laughing. His horse just died on the side of the road. "The one day I don't have my truck, I take the horse out, and this happens. I lost the alternator in my truck. Seems the horse's alternator went out, too."

"Where can I bring you, friend," Mr. Deer asks. I scooch over to the middle, so the man can get into the truck.

"My house is just down the road, and feel free to call me James."

"I'm Mr. Deer, and this is Lori. I'm minding her for the day for her brother."

James says hello and gives directions to his home. It's only a couple of miles away, and it's an old farmhouse. There's a barn out back, where he keeps chickens, sheep and the horse. Well, there's no horse now. She died on the edge of a tobacco field. That stuff really does kill.

He offers us some apple cake, so Mr. Deer and I go inside. James puts the cake on small white plates, and it has apples, cinnamon, and nutmeg. It's delicious. I look around the kitchen and see a Whirlpool refrigerator. There's even a phone, which James uses to call someone about his horse. I'm confused, because I thought the Amish didn't use modern things. He told Mr. Deer and me that he's a Mennonite, and they're not always as strict as the Amish. I figured they were all the same, but I also used to think all Indians wore feathers in their hair, and Mr. Deer doesn't wear feathers.

"Oh, what tribe are you from," James asks Mr. Deer.

"I'm Iroquois."

"Do you prefer if people call you Native American, or Indian, or Iroquois," James asked.

"I prefer to be called Alan," Mr. Deer smiles, and James laughs. "Although everyone just calls me Mr. Deer, just like my young friend here does."

"Yes, you said you were watching her. So, you live with your brother," James asked me. "Why not your parents?"

"Our dad died." I don't tell him anymore, and I ask about his horse instead. "I wonder if your horse was scared before she died."

"It was just a horse," James shrugged.

Before we leave, I said thank you for the cake, and James gives me a slice to bring home to Eddie. It's wrapped up in a tea towel with white and blue checks. I hold it very carefully because the pickup truck is very bumpy.

"Do you think animals get scared, Mr. Deer," I asked.

"I do, Lori. They can be happy, sad or angry, just like you and me. But there are a lot of people like James, who don't believe animals can have emotions."

The rest of the afternoon was quiet. We returned books to the library, and then we had lunch. Mr. Deer needs to eat soon, and we were going to eat at my brother's restaurant, but it's very busy. We go back to Mr. Deer's apartment instead, and he makes us a couple of hamburgers, and cooks them on the stove in an iron skillet. He puts a slice of white cheese on each one, and the cheese gets all melty. I put butter on the sesame seed buns, and he toasts them on another pan. I eat my hamburger with lots of mustard, lettuce and a juicy tomato slice. The table in the kitchen is small and covered in stuff so we eat in the living room on the couch. It starts to rain hard outside, and it gets dark, and I can barely see outside. I see our reflections in the window.

Eddie comes home around six, and I say thank you to Mr. Deer for the nice day, and my brother and I go back upstairs to our apartment. He makes chicken salad for supper, and when we finished, I told Eddie I had a special dessert just for him. I unwrap the slice of apple cake and give it to my brother on a saucer.

"This is amazing! Where did you get it, Lori?"

"James. His horse died, and we gave him a ride home," I explained, and I told Eddie about my day.

Underground
James L. Kaiser

I'm taking my daily commute home from work on the subway. It's late at night and a long way before my stop, so I have headphones on over my ears so that it looks like I'm listening to tunes. Honestly, my iPod's not even on—the battery's dead—but I find people generally won't try to talk to me if they assume they'll have to go out of their way to get my attention. I get to hear fascinating conversations this way, and oftentimes the subway chatter lulls me to sleep until my stop is announced on the tinny loudspeaker overhead.

Tonight, though, I've downed an energy drink too many and am wide awake. There aren't too many others riding right now, so most people are sitting in the gray plastic seats. Their bodies sway and jolt as the train slows and speeds up again. They are unfazed, engrossed in their cell phones or else out cold. One or two stand, though, perhaps unused to the idea of sitting next to strangers. The fluorescent lights from above are casting a slightly greenish tint onto everyone's faces. Purple and white sparks skitter past the black windows across from me as the train screeches to a graceless grating halt at the next stop.

Dozens of passengers board and suddenly all the seats in sight are occupied by tired and cranky commuters with bags under their bloodshot eyes. Now people are standing shoulder to shoulder, their annoyance palpable as they try to avoid touching. Perfume and cologne mingle with sweat all around. I close my eyes and try to nap for a few minutes. I finally feel myself dozing off as the train nears the next stop, but I soon find my eyes snapping wide open again as a woman's voice cries out in outrage above the even din. I look over down the aisle to my left to see a small twenty-something Asian woman wearing a magenta-colored cocktail dress and sparkling silver heels spinning around to face the tall, lanky man of similar age standing behind her. She is shouting angrily at him in what sounds to me like Mandarin; I can't make out a word. The man is raising his eyebrows and shrugging, feigning a look of innocence. The woman is still shouting at him, her brow curling down as her face flushes. The man just shakes his head back and forth, holding back laughter. Now the subway is stopping and he steps forward as to make way for the door. The woman plants herself in his path, forcing him to stop. She looks him in the eye as she slaps him stiffly across the face. She steps aside as the door opens; he walks outside with a smirk on his lips and a handprint emblazoned on his cheek.

The Simplicity of Dried Apricots
An Excerpt
G.R. Weslo

The Farm; a Beginning

My name is Randolph Jones Denton, but for as long as I can remember everyone has simply called me Jones. I was born on September 17, 1890, in Cardigan, Wisconsin. I am an old man now, and one reaching the end of his life, and so I have decided to look back at what I have lived and with who. The foremost of my lessons learned being that what happens in this world matters more on who it happens to and with, while less on what it actually was that happened. I was never a perfect man, and I made my mistakes, at times I was a bad man, but many of us can admit to that. Look as much as you can and will seldom find as many who was only good in life. I have lived for a long time and have seen the world change around me in wild and wondrous ways, but that is not to say always good ways. I have seen many wars and been in some, I have seen tyrants rise and fall with the next never seeing he is his predecessor, and I have felt love bloom and die in my hands. In thinking about the life I have lived, it makes little sense to me that it had such a humble beginning, a lentil farm in the heartland of a then young country.

When I was a young boy, having grown many years ago, I would wonder where the feeling of longing comes from. Why it was that a man would ache from an invisible force and allow it to control him on his decisions in life and in love. It was not until I was an older man, looking back with a steadfast hindsight that I was able to analyze my life for what it was. I, in my thoughts, would often compare myself to my father or grandfather, though never quite sure of which it would have been better to be like. Unthreatening and normal men that pursued normal lives and lived long and normal existences they were not more but notes within my childhood. My grandfather would sit on the porch and look with a piercing melancholy at the fields of the family farm. He seemed to look at what was and not is. Quietly humming to himself in between sips of whiskey and drags on hand-rolled cigarettes, he would give sermons on life and what he felt was important. To him a man's legacy was immutable, it was what people lived and died for. The farm I grew and worked on held not only my name but forefather's name. To my grandfather, this farm was his legacy and never let you forget what that meant. When I was around four, on a slow and rainy day, I was sitting on my grandfather's lap my grandmother sewing and looking at her grandson and husband lovingly. My grandfather told me to walk over to the front door of the house and look as to the tree fifty-so feet away. It was an oak tree that stretched high next to the large wooden gate adorned with the family name. When I could see it, I looked back to my grandfather and told him, he said to me that tree was his because he planted it, and he asked me to look out the lake two hundred feet from the tree and off to the side. I did and as I could see it, he got up to stand next to me, holding me next to him with a sense of guidance and wisdom he told me that the lake was his too, because he bought the land it rested on. Finally, he told me to turn around and look at the room we were in, and he asked me whose room this was. With a twinge of uncertainty, I answered that it was his. He chuckled and walked into the living room again. He said that this house was his to live in and one day it would be mine to live in, but it was not truly his because it was his grandfather who in fact had built it, and that it would always belong to his grandfather, if nothing else, out of respect.

I respected my grandfather until the day he died, in my eleventh year, but I never lived in that old farmhouse after I left at eighteen. It was not because I didn't like it, it was because it was not my legacy, the same way that that oak tree or lake was not my grandfather's legacy. A man's legacy was what he did, not what he had. My legacy was Luna, and the time that I spent with her. It was the only worthy aspect of my life worth telling, but to tell you about Luna I have to tell you how I came to know her and how it came to fall apart. I would say that an instrumental part of my life was when I met a woman that held herself in a uniquely guarded fashion. She was reserved in her life, keeping the deepest parts of herself right where they sat. I was a skeptical man when I met her, very sure of myself and of life in general. But there always requires a level of pull to move a nail from wood.

Columbia's Walls

I was nineteen years old when I met Luna. We attended the same school and as fate may have it, if you believe in that idea, we were drawn together. It wasn't by any intense or tumultuous actions either. She simply needed a book. I was working in the cataloging department, a job I thought would allow me to focus on my studies but turned out to be filled with tedious filing and shelving. On a particularly humid summer day, I was cataloging the new shipment of books that had arrived earlier that week. The sweet smell of old glue and my boss's pipe tobacco wafted through the halls. The hum of traffic and a light breeze drifted in from the windows, and I could feel my eyes heavy all that day. She came in early in the afternoon, looking for a book on the native population of some Polynesian island chain for a paper she had been putting off for a while now. She approached me with a level of excitement that shocked me out of my dulling concentration within the books. I don't particularly know what it was about that woman, but I was almost instantly intrigued with her. Her broad smile framing white square teeth, and her auburn hair bouncing in long loops around her face and shoulders painted a beautiful and captivating picture. At first, I was lost for words, a situation I seldom found myself in.

Looking at her in this old building made her seem out of place, as if she was a figment of my mind I plucked from some recess and dropped into my ever dulling job and life. I wanted to know her, at the extent of my desire was to know her, and to know about her. I found myself evaluating everything that was about life. What I did and more so what I didn't. Even as a young man I could recognize the mistakes that I had made in my past. Mistakes, being normal in life and not foreign to anyone, were an aspect of mine that I attempted to avoid. My naturally coarse nature made mistakes an unsettling affair. I preferred to make choices in life and not mistakes, the only real distinction between the two being how you feel about them. Knowing what my life was like, and more thinking I knew life itself, I planned to simply give her the book and be on with the rest of my shift. But as it happens something deep in my mind had an idea, a bad idea and one that I knew would lead to more options for mistakes. I began to talk to the woman, commenting on the ambition of her paper, and making light, small talk about the ever-increasing heat this summer had been experiencing. I decided within that moment that I liked Luna, and that liking Luna was one of the parts of my life that would matter the most. I made the choice to talk to Luna and to get to know her that day. Looking back at my life in review, I can see why. I can also say, knowing how my life unfolded, that I made the right choice.

Love, to me, was a confusing topic of thought. I could

never bring myself to define it and I don't think that it was because of any lacking vocabulary. I could only ever make comparisons to what love seemed like to me, what represented love. I never felt that there was a more true representation of love than in a painting that I saw on a holiday to New York; it was of a returning captain from the some terrible war, the only of his platoon to return. His wife held him in her arms as he sobbed onto her summer dress. I found this painting so enrapturing because I could not only feel the pain that was shown on his face but the love that was seen on her and in how his wife held him. To her, he was strong and brave and most of all human. To be seen as human means so much to people, we seem to forget that in our daily dealings. We are simply humans that are confused and humans that don't want to be confused. There were many people that passed me through in my life, and even more that passed me by, that's not a slight on them or on anyone really I am guilty of sins and of suffering. Contrapasso. The boring nature of social interaction rarely held my attention. My whole life I could hear my mother in my head speaking of my aloof nature and how it would come to haunt me in my old and lonesome age. There were women, but none ever held my gaze more than that of Luna. I can't bring myself to say that I loved her, or even confirm that what I felt was indeed love, but I do know that what I felt was a unique brand to her and to her alone.

For a time, as a young man, working on my father's lentil farm I began to convince myself that being a farmer would be an appropriate occupation for me. I felt at peace with myself and with the world while I was out in the fields. The cool bite of the early Wisconsin spring during harvest and the tending in the fall was to me a treasured time. My father was a man set in his ways and one that was sure of life, regardless of his experience in it. My father was so set in the idea that I would attend college. Without consulting me he had decided it, and while at first I was unsure of attending a university within the city I soon warmed to the idea. My first trip into the city I found myself confused and taken aback by the caustic nature of all that was around me. As I began to sink into the routine of the bustle and smog that surrounded the university, I found myself learning to like it. I settled on studying literature and found myself at home within Columbia University. Books provided interest for me and writing allowed me to explore the creative aspects of my mind and began to develop what came to be found as a natural talent. The discovery of the world outside of the farm, made me evaluate my prior thoughts and commitments. By the time I was twenty-two the allure that a famous life held no longer pulled me with its siren's song.

A professor during my freshman year posited a question for us. If we were to return to our hometowns and experience life after our first year in college, would it perhaps be different? Would it still hold the attention that it did of our childhood? Most of the students scoffed off the idea and thought that there would be no difference, save for of course the location of the beds in which they slept. I had not planned to return to the farm that year, though I longed to see the fields and in my homesick longing did miss my family. The logistics of returning to my home in Cardigan, Wisconsin proved to weigh on my patience and funds. I was wary of making the venture to Wisconsin; the world was still adolescent in its dealings with the people that traveled it. The hardened cowboys and ruffed outlaws made a near cross-country trip one to be careful of. I did return to home though, sure that it would be different as my professor proposed and I felt that I could not disservice myself in missing this learning experience. I was met with a timid reception, my father commenting on how he was using his money to give me an education and not to shuttle me across the world. I held my tongue deciding not to argue the fact that the carriage I had rented was nothing luxurious of the sort, and that I had only barely made it back to the home-like fields of my past. Conversing with my younger brother on the how the times were changing in the cities, and sure of myself when declaring that the heartland would soon pump with steam engines and coal I amazed my family with the wonders that was the modern city. Soon a timid welcome became uproarious but I found that they wanted to hear not of or about me but more of what I had seen in my travels. I told my stories and in that time wasn't much more than a treasured radio program.

I filled my stomach with my mother's cooking but still found myself longing for the baked breads found in Irish bakeries overfull with tenants or the bite of espresso peddled by immigrants on a dirty street. The city had taken my heart and made me appreciate its unfitted and licentious nature. The biggest difference I found on my return was that there was a quiet noise to the country, that all that was in this town was so quiet that it became loud. I found it deafening to hear the bugs and the animals and the creaking of the wooden house we slept in at night. It was two days into my return that I decided not to ever venture back to the farm. I could not contain my contempt to the boring nature of everything around me and more so I found myself aching to return to the halls of Columbia and the museums at night. As the summer months dragged, I spent my days working in the fields, tilling to keep my mind from the monotony of the hum. It was in those days that I really began to think about love, and longing. I had, to my best knowledge, never experienced love and was beginning to desire to feel something of it. Writing in my journal, that I was almost never seen without, I would detail everything I could about such a feeling and about why such a feeling was so internal to the human spirit. As an old man and as I look back, I can see the foolish nature of most my ways but no more than those days I spent on my return to Cardigan, Wisconsin. I had begun to plan and theorize what love was before I had ever felt it and before Luna had walked into my life. I likened my adolescent ignorance to that of the men whispering about that long railroad or those outlaws, sure of a future that was ending in their hands.

The Execution of Fredrick Harper McElhenny
Jayson Robert Ducharme

The gallows stand like some dismal mast in the center of the courtyard. The guard to my right, Dekker, holds tight to my forearm. While he's good at keeping his face stony, his eyes tell me that he doesn't want to go through with this. Over the past three years, he and I have gotten exceptionally close. It's been the longest three years of my life, and he's been one of the few rays of light to comfort me on this journey. I think he truly believes that I didn't do it.

Not like that matters, of course. It'll take a lot more than the hunch of a sixty-seven-year-old prison beat cop with arthritis in both hands to pardon me. No mistake can be made by this point: I'm going to die today. I've lived for twenty-seven years, and all that's left is about five minutes.

All of this—Dekker, the gallows, the sound of gospels singing from the prison chapel—hits me at once and I stagger, nearly falling over. Dekker manages to catch me by the arm and pulls me to my feet.

"C'mon, bud," he tells me, "I'm right here."

With a light tug, he gets me going again, towards that arch of wood with the rope dangling down it like some macabre uvula. The front of my shirt is wet with hot perspiration and I wish I'd taken a leak earlier when I still had a chance.

I am going to die a criminal. No one will grieve me. I have no mother or father—Mom died birthing me and Dad went and abandoned me when I was about ten. I never had any sisters or brothers, no cousins or nothing that I know of. I was raised from stranger to stranger. I am nobody's child, nobodies relative. My fate—who I am and what I will die as was sealed the moment that Judge's gavel hammered home.

Yet—no. No, I don't accept that! I'm not a criminal! This

was an abstraction that was imposed on me, purely circumstantial! I'm a car mechanic! I'm anything in the world but a criminal!

It's like being trapped. My cries don't touch any ear that cares. "There goes that awful Freddy McElhenny," they'll say while reading tomorrow morning's paper. "Good riddance—leeches on society, is what he and all those others down in Concord are. The world will be better off without them, the whole lot of them."

I remember I once grieved to Dekker over this, perhaps two weeks ago. I knew my day was coming and he heard me crying in my dark cell. Thank God it was only him on watch that night—if it was Levesque, he probably would have harassed me. Dekker brought over a chair and sat before my cell, his shape dark against the corridor light, and I sat up on my cot and talked with him.

I told him the worst thing about this whole mess wasn't the fact that I was going to die, but it was that my death would determine who I am. Some people spend their whole lives trying to make something of themselves. Doctors, lawyers, teachers, and firefighters. I wound up fixing cars. That's still something, isn't it? I was Freddy-Fix'em-Up. I helped people get to work, go on dates, take their kids to the park. I did something for society. That's who I am. Ever since I was sentenced to die, though . . . I am no longer Freddy-Fix'em-Up. I am Freddy the criminal, Freddy the killer. I spent my whole life trying to do right by people, and without my knowing, without any premeditation on my end, the Powers that Be decided that I needed to die a bad guy.

Dekker listened to me rant, tried to consolidate me by quoting Dostoevsky—telling me that earthly and divine justice are not one in the same. I couldn't take it seriously. It meant nothing to me. Still doesn't. It doesn't matter how much of a good person you are. When you least expect it, the world will decide for you what you are.

I'm being lead up the wooden steps onto the platform of the gallows now. Speaking of Dostoevsky, that son of a bitch got lucky. Imagine that, a pardon right when they had him tied to the mast, rifles ready. Then he gets off with a pardon, to live another day. Now everyone knows him as this hotshot famous writer. He's been dead for seventy years but he's still very much alive through his accomplishments. He didn't die a criminal. Where the hell is my redemption? Why would anything good happen in this rotten world?

They're tightening that awful rope around my neck now. I can see clouds in the sky, and a sudden fondness for my body comes over me. I should have drunk and smoked less. I shouldn't have spent so much time indoors or wallowing in misery. I should've told that girl at the counter some years back that she was pretty. I should've donated to charity more when those church kids came by. I should've adopted a dog from a shelter before they turned him into glue. I should've done a lot of things, but I didn't.

What if this is something I deserve? I didn't ever commit the crime they say I did, but what if I misspent the way that I lived my life? I know I haven't been perfect—I rolled in the hay with other women, I stole drinks from the liquor store, and I once broke a feller's nose over a well-deserved insult while bull drunk. No, if I had the chance now, I'd give all the money I have to the poor, and I'd track down that sorry bastard whose nose I broke and I'd pay his hospital fee. I'd swear off drinking for life and I'd tell every girl she was beautiful. Please, I'd do anything to show that I'm still a good person who's worth a damn. Please just give me that chance.

The crows are calling, I can hear them. The gospels in the chapel have ceased. "Any last words?" the guy at the lever asks me. I can see Dekker, standing straight with his hands laced neatly in front of him, looking at me, doing his best to keep his composure. I want to tell him how good he was to me, but I'm all choked up. Not like this. Not like this . . .

I say nothing, and they put that hood over me and the world goes dark. The last time I was ever happy was when I was about nine years old, just before my dad up and vanished like smoke. He took me out on the lake in town in his little rowboat to go fishing. I caught this big son of a bitching catfish that nearly tore my arms off when I tried to reel him in. Dad grabbed the fishing pole as I held on to it, and together we reeled the fish in. Once we had that little bastard out of the water, we both laughed as it struggled helplessly in the air at the end of the line. I shouted in joy, like I'd just conquered the whole damn world. Dad said, "You did it, kid."

I wonder if they have fishing where I go. Maybe I'll—

How to Ruin Steak
Casey Kimball-Marfongelli

A bottle of ketchup is squeezed gently to push the sauce out of its container. Its stressed sides are compressed by the grip of a middle-aged woman sitting on a barstool—the swivel kind someone might find in a diner. A man sits just two seats away, watching her, waiting for her to finish so he may ask for it to put on his burger and fries. She was putting ketchup on her steak, which was gross. Both the customers desire to make their meals tastier, adding the simple sauce to their food.

The bottle appears full due to the translucent texture of its casing. It had enough visibility to be seen through, that way the staff knows when it needs to be refilled—this one did not. It was more than half full—maybe three-quarters—and would be used until it was probably about half full—or half empty. The bottle was one of those refillable ones that are typically in cartoons or films with scenes taking place in diners. The one like that episode of *Spongebob* where the guy squirts mayonnaise directly into his mouth from a white bottle—except this one is red. It can be noted that the bottle has likely been around for years, having crusted bits around the top that have dried from lack of cleaning. However, it appears as if the bottle had been wiped down many times to look at least somewhat clean.

The woman is old enough to be considered middle-aged but not old enough to be considered old. Her blonde hair remains vibrant due to her various trips to the salon, maintaining the color that was once natural until time takes it away from her. She was wrapped in a casual sweater that lacked any noticeable features—simple, how she liked her appearance to be. It fit her well, portraying a look that took minimal effort but was still pleasing to the eye. She did not dress to impress, but simply to blend in and be left to her own business.

The woman, although unknown to the man watching her, is currently dealing with the following:

- A cramp in her forearm from holding the bottle at an awkward angle.

- A slight pain in her stomach as she had missed lunch—one that would soon go away once she was finished with dinner.

- No more battery in her phone—which is the worst.

- Also, her marriage is failing.

The man is eager at this point, waiting to put the condiment on his burger so that he may eat, tip the waitress—who was very cute, he noticed—and go home to his dog, Edgar. The man has less distinct hair; although it is full and far from balding, it is not kept up with very well. His face, however, is clean shaven, showing his well-structured jawline. He has a similar style in terms of clothing, wearing a casual button-down, collared shirt. A thick, silver watch was worn on his right wrist. Aside from waiting, the man is also dealing with some things which are unknown to the woman:

- He has a bruise on his shin from bumping it on his desk at work when he stood up to use the restroom.

- Edgar is sick and needs to have full attention as much as possible.

- He has to fart.

- While waiting for his food, he just watched a video on his phone of a car accident involving the death of a child no older than twelve—he thought of his own daughter.

The man taps his fingers on the table in a rhythmic fashion, playing the drumline to Foghat's "Slow Ride." He taps the ceramic dish with a steel knife that represents the hitting of a cymbal. He glances at the waitress as she walks past, having dropped his meal in front of him in the process. The smell of his burger fills the immediate air around him, causing him to salivate more and more. The woman shakes the bottle a bit, mixing up the ingredients that had settled inside. After this, she disperses some onto her steak, which is cooked well done, and more onto her dish for her fries.

The man wants the ketchup and she is done with it. "Excuse me, may I?" He says with a gesture. She pushes it over to him and he takes it. He puts ketchup on his burger but not too much. He also puts ketchup on his plate for his fries. The two eat in silence because they are not together. Their meals are different. The man will enjoy his meal, but the woman won't.

The diner is filled with pleasant light emanating from old-fashioned, artificial candles suspended on brass holders on the walls. Each table, lining the walls, held one of these fake candles which provides a portion of light for anyone within a few feet of it. Alone, these lights only shined enough for their respective tables, but, together, they lit up the entirety of the dining room. The inside of the building appears to be glowing through the power of individual sources of light.

The man puts the ketchup down after using it and turns his attention back to the woman, "That's unique," he gestures towards her plate.

"I don't like it either."

"Why'd you get it then?"

Later, the woman would leave the room without a hundred-dollar bill—about eighty percent of which would be a tip. The man would feel sad, in a sense, as if he was in some type of nineties movie where the potential love of his life just walked out the door and he only exchanged minimal words with her. His curiosity of her words and actions would truly grasp him, telling him to chase her out the door, offer her a drink down the road at the Stumble In bar, offer her a ride home, give her a phone number—something. His dreams would seem ridiculous, so all he would have is a memory of the few words exchanged and the various looks on her face as she took an already ruined steak and made it worse somehow.

"I'm losing my mind," she said.

A Piece of Us
Lauren Ashley

When Bree pulled into the church parking lot, she bit her lip as she searched for a spot to park. Her nerves were beginning to show, and she questioned herself for even going to the wedding in the first place. It wasn't until she received the beautiful, floral invitation in the mail that she found out Jesse was getting married. As she opened the seal and untied the ribbon, her heart had melted into her hands. Bree and Jesse had been best friends since they met in kindergarten, and they were in love up until a year ago.

Their relationship was always good, and they rarely ever fought, but time had pushed a wedge between them and they lost sight of one another in the midst of their separate daily lives. Bree was working as an editor for an online news company, and Jesse got his hands dirty underneath cars all day. What was once extraordinary had turned into the ordinary and Jesse decided to move on. He wanted more excitement, but Bree was content with their simple life together. She begged him to stay, but it hadn't changed his mind. She struggled with his decision and tried her hardest to stay strong for the next nine months. She missed him dearly, and when Jesse ran through Bree's mind as a thought, it would tug at her heartstrings. She still hadn't dated anyone since they broke up, and didn't want to. She loved Jesse too much to believe that they wouldn't end up together, or at least that was what she thought until she got invited to his wedding.

After a few weeks of debating whether or not to attend, followed by a few weeks of deciding what to wear, the day of the wedding had finally come. As Bree slipped her car under a tree in the far end of the parking lot, she hurriedly made her way inside the church. The pews were full of people, some faces she knew and others she did not. She tucked her dress underneath her as she slid into a row on the groom's side. She looked around for Jesse, but he was not in sight. He hadn't returned any of her phone calls since they parted ways, but she thought about him every day. Her stomach did flips while her mind raced back and forth to their relationship. She had made the decision to go to the wedding because she cared about him and respected him. They were lifelong friends, aside from everything else, and they shared something infinite that Jesse wasn't aware of. At that moment, it was a battle for Bree to suppress her feelings of sadness and discomfort. She didn't *want* to be there, sitting in a pew. She wanted to be the one walking down the aisle.

The quiet voices of the guests had gradually diminished to whispers and then silence, as the wedding music began to play. Everyone shifted in their seats to watch as the beautifully dressed bridesmaids were escorted down the aisle by groomsmen. Bree looked towards the altar and caught a glimpse of Jesse. Her hands started to shake and her lips began to quiver as she stared at the handsome man her heart still belonged to. She could feel an overwhelming rush of emotion build up in her eyes, and begin to slide down her face. She brushed a tear from her cheek and followed along with everyone as they stood up and turned towards the door.

The silence in the church was overwhelmingly loud as the bride appeared in the doorway. The white elegance pierced Bree's eyes. The woman was tall and thin, and had perfectly curled blonde hair resting on her shoulders. She was draped in lace and pearls, and a smile from ear to ear. As she began to walk down the aisle, Bree's hopes began to disintegrate. This woman looked genuinely happy, and as she gazed towards Jesse, he did too.

Bree sat with her hands clenched together in her lap

throughout the entire ceremony, and quickly exited the church, camouflaged by the crowd of guests, when it had ended. She felt relief when she had made it back to her car without being noticed. She unlocked the door and grabbed a cigarette from the pack in her center console. She lit the tip, and moved to lean up against the tree. She could see in the distance, all the happy faces of the people that were gathered there waiting to leave for the reception. She couldn't help but feel jealous, as she took a long slow drag. But as more and more guests began to drive away, she flicked her cigarette and got in the car. In the rearview mirror, she could see the empty baby-seat in the back, and checked her phone to make sure she hadn't missed any calls.

On the five-minute drive to the reception hall, she blasted her favorite song and sang it as loud as she could. She felt comfort in this and it temporarily eased her nerves. But that relief slowly turned back to anxiety when she finally arrived. Her plan was to go in, chug a beer, say congratulations and then leave. Simple. It started out that way, but after the beer, the plan faltered. While standing at the bar, she unexpectedly made eye contact with Jesse. She snapped her head in the opposite direction, but he made his way over to her before she could escape. Her palms began to sweat, and she felt like she couldn't breathe.

"Bree . . . I'm so happy that you are here! How are you? I'm sorry that I haven't really been in touch, but as you can probably imagine, I've been pretty busy," Jesse stammered over his words as he spoke.

Bree had an urge to burst into tears and she fought herself to hold back.

"Congrats Jesse. I'm really happy for you . . ." and with the pain soaring through her, she clenched her teeth and forced out a smile. "Unfortunately, though, I can't stay. I really should get home because, ya know, I've been pretty busy too. And maybe if you had ever returned my phone calls then you might know that, but you don't so, whatever." She couldn't help but ramble, and she couldn't control her emotions. She was filled with so many things that she wanted to say, but she prided herself on being too proper to do that at a time like this.

Jesse grabbed Bree's shoulder as she started to turn away from him, "No, you can't leave. I want to catch up, and I really want you to meet Rachel."

"I'm sorry Jesse, but I have to go get Stella. The sitter can only stay until seven, and it's already six-thirty," and as she ended her sentence, her thoughts caught up to her. She cupped her mouth as it fell open in realizing that she had just mentioned what she had been hiding.

"Who is Stella? Wait, you have a kid?" He looked completely dumbfounded.

But without a word, Bree threw Jesse's hand off her shoulder and ran towards the door. She bumped into a few people as she made her way to her car. Before she could get the key in to unlock it, Jesse was standing behind her.

"Bree! What is going on with you? Tell me, please!" Jesse's voice chilled Bree's veins and flowed directly into her chest. She couldn't help but love him and want him. She missed him dearly and was so distraught by being at his wedding that she felt like she was going out of her mind.

"Why, Jesse? Since when do you care about me? You have ignored me for almost a year now and moved on faster than I could even imagine. Did you ever even love me? Move out of the way. I have to go pick up Stella!" Bree's entire body was shaking as she fought to pull her car door open against Jesse's weight.

Jesse was intent on getting an answer.

"Just tell me who Stella is and then you can leave," he pleaded.

With tears pouring from her eyes, Bree looked deep into Jesse's and said, "She's our daughter."

Shattered
An Excerpt
Kate Johnston

Vivian watched Maryann twist her wedding ring, remembering the day in the hospital when her parents renewed their wedding vows. The cancer made her father too weak to slip the ring on her mother's finger, and she helped him. After he died, Jen buried the ring in the garden. Since then, a single blossom of a rare flower species known as the Lone Wolf grew there. It survived under any circumstance, alone, never dying. Not even in the harsh winters.

Jen helped Maryann to her feet. "I'll show you the guest room. Vivi, I'll be back in a minute to do your hair."

Vivian listened to Maryann's stilettos click through the house, a deliberate, tense rhythm that got under her skin.

The screen door swung open with gusto. Vivian turned in surprise.

Maryann's mother-in-law, Gussie, burst into the house. She was wearing her usual attire of tennis whites. "Where's Maryann?" Without waiting for an answer, Gussie marched through the house, shouting, "Maryann, dammit! What the hell you doing?"

Vivian flinched. She'd known Gussie forever, and never had she heard her scream an obscenity.

She heard her mother's voice. "Gussie. You've no right yelling your head off in my home. Please leave."

Vivian went upstairs. Worry stuck in her throat like a sand burr as Gussie screamed at Maryann. Maryann was in tears, covering her face with her broken hand.

"How dare you drag your dirty laundry here," Gussie admonished. "Come back and work things out with your husband."

Maryann brushed past Vivian and went downstairs. Gussie started to follow her, but Jen caught her arm.

"Gussie, you and I need to talk. Vivi, please check on Maryann."

Vivian tracked Maryann by the echo of her stilettos. She found her in the living room, which had been Vivian's father's favorite room. The leather chair and the shelves of books still smelled like his cologne, no matter how many mothballs her mother threw around.

Maryann paced the room like a caged animal. Her hands were unraveling her damp tissue and crumpling it into a ball.

"I shouldn't have come here," Maryann said. "I've jeopardized your friendship with Gussie."

"We can help you and still be good neighbors with Gussie," Vivian said.

Maryann continued to pace and worry her tissue. Vivian thought about the time she found Charlie by the saltmarsh, sitting there like a broken-winged bird. His father was drunk and getting rough, and Charlie ran to avoid a beating.

"When he's sober, I'll go back. I need to let him cool down. If I'm there, he'll start hitting. And they'll take me away again." Charlie's face soured. "Like a foster home is any safer."

Vivian brought Charlie home. Her house overlooked land where great blue herons cavorted. He walked beside her, slope-shouldered and dark. His jeans and sneakers were soaked from having sat in the marshes.

She led him through the back part of her house, to the laundry room. She left him there while she ran up to the dark bedroom that her mother didn't sleep in anymore and grabbed random articles of her father's clothing. She handed Charlie the stack. "Pick something."

Then, Vivian found her mother in the study, paying bills.

"I brought home a friend," Vivian said.

Without asking the name of the friend, Jenn replied, "I'll set another place at the table."

Charlie stayed for four days. Jenn went to his dad and explained they were taking care of Charlie until he felt better. Vivian wasn't sure how she'd worded it but had a feeling she laid it out in simple terms. *If you can't treat your boy right, you're going to lose him again. Get a grip. Stop drinking.* Just like that night when her mother buried the ring and said, *Vivi, your dad died, and now it's just the two of us. We'll be okay, but we have to work together.*

As Vivian watched Maryann struggle to regain her composure, she realized Maryann had lied. She didn't act shocked enough. She acted like Charlie did that day by the saltmarsh, someone who understood the magnitude of the trouble she was in.

"He's done this before. Hasn't he?"

Maryann snuffled. "He's under a lot of pressure."

"How bad?" Vivian eyed the windows. Her nerves spiked. Gussie was here, but Foss wasn't? Why hadn't he come to get his wife? Why was Gussie here?

"We used to have a kitten."

Vivian swallowed around the lump in her throat. She watched Maryann stroke her broken bone with force.

"The kitten was playing with his cufflinks. Lost one of them. He picked up that little guy and threw him." She tapped her forehead. "Smashed into the wall."

Vivian's stomach dropped.

"Once, I found Gussie in the bathroom. Her arm was cut up. She said he'd pushed her, and she put out her arm to stop from falling. She went through the window."

"We need to tell my mom." Suddenly Vivian didn't feel safe in her own home. Two battered women had sought shelter there, and the abuser was next door.

She grabbed Maryann's good hand. They headed upstairs when Gussie and her mother met them on the landing. Jen looked stricken.

"Vivi. Grab the cell. I'll get the car keys."

Gussie must have confessed, Vivian thought. They all hurried downstairs, but Vivian ran, feeling flames at her back. Her father's voice in her head, *Stay calm, think, be careful.*

She burst into the kitchen and pulled up short. Maryann's husband, Foss, blocked her way. Dressed in his Armani suit and shiny shoes, he held a gun. The black metal matched his black stare.

"Where's my wife?"

Vivian backed away.

"Foss!"

Jen's voice cut through the room with authority, surprising Foss enough that he wavered in his stance. In one breath, Jen was between Foss and Vivian.

"Where's my wife?"

Vivian could see his face over her mother's shoulder. His hair, normally combed back and glossy with oil, was disheveled. His dark eyes moved with agitation. She could smell him, too. A mixture of sweat and Polo, slick nerves. Handing over Maryann might save everyone else, but it'd mean certain death for Maryann. On the other hand, protecting Maryann was fruitless. Foss held a gun, reminding her he'd been stationed in Afghanistan. He'd seen brutal action, been awarded medals for bravery. He knew how to kill and how to survive.

"Foss, I've known you a long time. You plow our driveway for God's sake. You drove me to the hospital when Danny—" Jen paused, her voice breaking. "You don't need a gun. Not with me."

"You could've let me know she was with you. Instead of letting me shoot up the bar."

"You did *what?*"

"She always runs to the bar. Whenever things get stressful. But tonight she came here." His eyes roamed the kitchen. "Why'd she come here instead?"

Vivian clutched her mother's arm. White heat penetrated her mind as she grew fearful for Maryann.

Floorboards creaked behind her. Vivian turned and saw Maryann and Gussie, holding each other up. Gussie was a pale green, the color of unripe pears. But Maryann was pink-faced beneath the fear and bruises.

"Foss, don't be angry with Jen. Please, put the gun away."

"Only if you come with me." His lips tightened. "You too, Mother. We're going home."

Vivian thought about Gussie's cut-up arm. The kitten. Maryann's injuries. Vivian buried her face in her mother's scrub top. God forgive us, Vivian prayed. Forgive us for letting them go back.

Sirens pierced the night. Vivian lifted her face. She looked out the window and the cedars let her watch two police cruisers pull into the Harding's driveway. He really did shoot up the bar, she thought.

"The police are looking for you, Foss," Jen said.

Vivian could see sweat breaking on his brow. What if the cops never think to look for him here?

He waved the gun erratically. "Sit down."

They sat on the floor against the cabinetry. Gussie moaned, and Jen leaned over, asking if she felt okay.

"Shut up, Jen," Foss growled, kicking her.

"Your mother . . ."

"She's fine." He dragged out a chair and straddled it, leaning his arms over the back. The gun dangled from his hand. "Let's play a game. Confess your biggest regret." He pointed to Vivian. "You first, pretty in pink."

Vivian stared at him. He's a maniac, she thought. Gussie

let out another moan. Vivian peered around her mother. Gussie's pale complexion now looked gray. Her eyes were dim, zoned out. "Mom," Vivian said urgently. "Gussie's . . ."

Suddenly, Gussie slumped over to the side, her head thudding on the wooden floor. Her hands fluttered to her heart, as if in prayer.

"Jesus! She's having a heart attack." Vivian's mother reached for Gussie, but Foss kicked her shoulder with his shiny shoe.

Jen grimaced, clutching her shoulder. "If I don't help her, she'll die."

"Then hurry along your answers. I'm waiting, Vivian."

Vivian's throat tightened. Considering what she was facing now, her regrets seemed laughable.

"Confess!" Foss screamed.

Vivian winced and said in a rush, "I didn't take care of Mr. Darcy. My parakeet. He died. I was too busy with my friends, and I forgot about him."

"A dead parakeet? That's the worst thing you've done?"

Vivian nodded. She'd kept one of his feathers, attached it to a clip and wore it in her hair.

Foss swiveled the gun. "Jen? What do you confess?"

Vivian noticed her mother was motionless. Vivian squeezed her hand. "Mom. Foss asked you a question."

"I heard him."

Vivian stole a glance at Foss. He tapped his gun against his Armani suit. His mouth played at the corners. He was enjoying himself, this stupid game.

"The longer you take, Jen, the worse my mother gets. She's right there, having a heart attack and you could help her. Play the game."

"The police will be here any minute."

"Obviously you have many regrets to choose from. Maryann, your turn while Jen takes her pick."

55

Maryann sniffed into the tissue. "I wish we hadn't moved in with your mother."

Foss narrowed his eyes. "That's what you regret? Not marrying me? Meeting me?"

Maryann's tissue was a mass of colors from her makeup, reminding Vivian of a Monet painting. "No, hon. I wish we'd gotten our own place. I think we'd have been happier."

"It's not too late," Jen said gently. "You still can make those plans. Where would you live?"

"Beacon Hill," Maryann said. "In one of those brownstones."

"We'd go to the theater," Foss added as though they'd dreamed about this before. "Picnic by the Charles River."

Vivian cautiously gazed at Gussie. The old woman was inert, her breathing shallow. She sensed her mother's anxiety and knew there wasn't much time left.

"That sounds lovely," Jen encouraged. "You could have a kitten."

Vivian drew in a sharp breath and cut her eyes to Maryann.

"Enough!" Foss jumped up and kicked the chair, sending it flying across the room. He swiped plates from the hutch and they crashed to the floor, breaking.

He strode over to Jen and pressed the gun to her temple. Vivian stifled a scream as the metal lodged against her mother's head.

"Five seconds, Jen. Five seconds to confess the worst thing you've done."

"Killing my husband," Jen said in a low, flat voice.

Vivian pulled back slowly. What did she say? Killing Daddy? No, she must be lying, to calm Foss. That must be it. Vivian watched Jen stare into Foss's stony face. She wasn't blinking, wasn't giving any sign she was lying.

Impossible. No way. Her mother didn't do terrible things. She was perfect. She knew how to knit and ride horses and

56

turn wedding rings into flowers.

Foss didn't seem repelled. Rather, his eyes glinted. "Go on."

Jen spoke in short sentences, while the gun remained on her head. "The cancer wouldn't go away. We couldn't afford his meds. We were about to lose the house. Everything. I had a daughter to raise."

"Basically, it came down between your daughter and your husband."

"Basically," she said through clenched teeth.

"You took away his chances. Watched him suffer. Let him die. And all this time you pretended to be the grieving widow."

He drew back and sat on his heels. He held his gun casually over his knee, like he was posing for a picture. "You're a murderer, Jen." He said it in awe, as though he'd met his hero.

"Foss. I played your game. Let me help Gussie."

"Sure, whatever."

Vivian's hands dropped from her mother's arm. She watched Jen crawl over Gussie's body and check her breathing.

Jen's eyes flicked over to Vivian. Her lips quivered and she whispered, "I'm sorry, Vivi. We wanted to protect you, give you a good life."

So, it was true. Tears filled Vivian's eyes. How was being without her father a good life? She had no chance without him, her strong father who taught her how to spot a saltmarsh sparrow and to love Shakespeare. He had more to give her, teach her, and she'd never know any of it. She looked away from her mother and glared at Foss. None of this would be happening if her father were here. Foss never would have held them up with a gun if her father were here.

"Foss." Maryann's voice was unsteady. "We can make it if

we run."

Foss blinked at his wife.

Maryann dabbed her eyes. "I have some money with me. And clothes." She stood up, indicating the pile of bags. "Right here, baby."

"Seriously?" he asked.

"We'll run. They'll never find us."

Dead Reckoning

Leo T.F. Martin

"Hatchet" Bill Williams held his colt pointed at the red-haired woman who sat with her back propped against a majestic pine. A battered Stetson lay a few feet from her, and blood flowed from her temple where they had managed to wing her. Rumor said that she had put down half a dozen men. Now she sat, her eyes glaring naked hatred back at him and his surviving partner, Jake Smalls.

Around them the brown husks of dead leaves and pine needles fluttered lazily in the late Autumn breeze, adding to the soft carpet that already covered the forest floor. "Brimstone Mills," he said, smiling as he tightened his finger on the trigger. Both men knew her by reputation. She was a killer and was supposed to be as fast as a burning rattler with that old gun she carried at her side.

Hatchet and Jake hadn't thought much about the lady lead-slinger before, until the day they had run into her in the two-bit saloon in that silver mining camp, and the missing third of their trio had called her out. That encounter had seen "Scratch" Johnson end up with a slug of lead in his belly and had left Hatchet and Jake as a duo. Unwilling to share their partner's fate, they had lit out, but the damned woman had been tracking them ever since.

She'd been trailing the pair for about a week, like Satan himself was holding a pitchfork to her backside. Then Jake had the idea of hiding in the woods and leaving the horses out where they could be seen. Then they could jump out and ambush their dogged pursuer when she came close.

They had waited the better part of a day for the bitch to turn up, and when she did, Hatchet could have sworn he saw a red flash come from her holster, right before her horse had

59

spooked and reared up. Jake had still been able to crease her, though, and now Hatchet had the drop on her. He still felt uneasy.

"You killed our friend, Brimstone," he said, taking a tentative step forward.

"Mah name is Chastity," the woman responded, wincing slightly at the pain in her temple. "And your friend needed killin.'"

"Don't matter," Hatchet replied, turning his head to spit. "But we ain't got no truck with you. Let's us call it even."

"No, Hatchet. We cain't," she said in a smooth, southern drawl. "Ah know what you piles of worm spit have done, and there ain't no lettin' go. Not now." In spite of her situation, the woman's words were as soft and cool as dirt on a fresh grave.

"You don't strike me as being in no position to determine that, right Jake?" he said, without casting his eyes over to his partner. He knew the twig-thin, scraggly bearded man was nodding behind his rifle. "Now maybe if you was to ask me nice . . ."

"Ah only ever begged one man," Chastity said, her deep green eyes suddenly burning. "And he went and let me live. His mistake. Besides," she turned the full fury of her gaze on the man in front of her, "them girls begged, and it didn't do them a lick of good, did it?"

Hatchet's blood froze. <u>How could she know?</u>

Things hadn't always been like this. When he had come out west from Boston, he had just been another tinhorn looking to make a fortune in the gold trade. There was tons of the stuff out here, so the stories went, just waiting to be picked up!

After six long months of trying, though, things had started to get desperate. That's when he had met Jake and Scratch. They hadn't had any more luck than him, so they had all decided that mining the valuables from lonely settlers was easier than breaking their backs working the land. Sometimes there were even "fringe benefits" like those twin daughters from their last job. Hatchet smiled, remembering their scared faces. They *had* begged.

Jake had wanted to let the victims go afterward, but Scratch protested, so did Hatchet. And That's how he got his moniker. It was a perfect scheme. If anybody came looking for a bunch of tenderfoot settlers, they would just find the pieces and figure it was Injuns. Worked like a charm. Until now.

Hatchet cleared his throat. "Way I see it, a dangerous criminal killed our friend, then tried to rob us on the trail, ain't that right, Jake?"

"Sure, Hatchet," came the other man's raspy voice. It was shaky.

"And nobody will say different." Hatchet's confidence was beginning to return now. He was the one holding the gun. "Just one thing I'm muddy on. How'd you manage to track us all this way?"

"Woman's intuition," Chastity spat.

Hatchet threw back his head and laughed. "That's a good one. I can see it on your tombstone now. 'Here lies Brimstone Mills, killed by woman's intuition!'" He and Jake laughed again, and then his eyes were pulled to the weapon at the woman's side.

"You know, they say you got that smoke-wagon from Lucifer his self, since you's so fast with it. Any truth to that?"

Chastity stared at him impassively.

"Mebbe I'll just see for m'self. Keep her covered, Jake." The other man nodded and Hatchet leaned in, holstering his pistol as he slid the gunslinger's from its worn leather sheath. Carefully, he turned it over in his hands. "Don't look so special to me," he said as he spun the cylinder.

"It belonged to mah husband," Chastity replied, a tiny smile coming to her face. "And he never did lahke for anybody else to touch it."

At that moment, there was a flash of red, and strange, glowing symbols appeared on the pistol's barrel as if carved in fire. It gave off an eerie, crimson glow that enveloped Hatchet's hand, and suddenly it felt like he was holding the business end of a branding iron. He screamed and dropped the gun, clutching at his still-smoking hand.

Chastity caught the glowing weapon neatly as it fell, cocking and firing it in a single motion. Jake toppled over dead.

Hatchet dropped to his knees. He had never felt pain like this in his whole life. Before him, the scarlet-haired shootist got to her feet, then calmly picked up her hat, beating it against her pant leg to brush the forest flotsam off before putting it on her head.

A few feet away, the outlaw could see the thin gray mist start to rise from the body of his former friend. It flowed toward the pistol, which began to draw it inside itself. Fearfully, Hatchet's eyes shifted from the gun to the woman. She was standing over him now, her arm glowing, the blood no longer running from her temple.

"Vengeance is mahne, sayeth the Lord," she said softly. "Those are pretty words." Chastity's smile broadened as she looked down at him, demon pistol aimed at his head. "But for some people, for the pain they've caused, vengeance ain't enough, is it? People lahke that, they need a <u>reckonin'</u>. And ah find, in those cases, the Almighty ain't none to particular who gets used as an instrument."

A delicate thumb pulled back the burning gun's hammer. "Give the Devil mah best," Chastity said, the smile falling from her face as softly as the leaves fluttering around them.

"No!" Hatchet screamed, as the hammer fell.

Just Off Main Street
Kari Nguyen

I turn the car out of the driveway and onto Pearl Street. Dad's sitting in the seat next to me, fumbling with the seat belt. I pretend not to notice. He likes to do things himself, to the extent that he's able. He can barely see at this point, but the basic things he can handle by feel, touch, memory.

"How's the temperature for you?" I ask, thankful to see that he finally has the seat belt fastened.

"It's fine, don't worry. I'll let you know," he says.

"So, where are we going? Florida?" I joke. "We can go wherever you like."

"Florida sounds nice," he says, "but I forgot to pack my bathing suit."

We both know we're headed towards Main Street, because it's where he's asked me to take him today.

"I'll take you out, Dad. Anywhere you want to go," I'd told him. And he wanted to drive down Main Street.

At the end of Pearl, I take a left.

"Ah yes, this must be—"

"Congress Street," I finish for him.

"That's right. It was on the tip of my tongue. Congress Street. You know I dated a girl who lived on Congress Street?"

"You did? When?"

"Oh, well, it would have been 1952."

"Isn't that around the time you met Mom?"

"She was my last girlfriend before your mother."

"Good to know," I say.

We drive on for a few minutes before he says, "Tell me everything you see."

"I will, Dad."

"I want to know what downtown looks like now. It's been so long since I've seen it."

"I know. I will. I promise."

It's been so long since I've seen it too.

I ask him, "Dad, do you remember when you used to take the whole family out driving?"

"Of course, I do. We'd all pile in the car and drive down this way."

"And you'd roll down the windows and blast your old music just to embarrass me."

"That doesn't sound like me!" he laughs, adding, "I could do it again if you like?"

"Very funny."

I realize how much I've missed him, missed this. I want to reach over and hold his hand, but I don't want to be awkward.

"Okay, Dad, we're coming up on Main Street. I'm about to stop at the light here, and then we'll pass through the rotary."

"Can you see the square?"

"I can."

"And?"

"Oh, right. Well, uh, there's the white gazebo, and walking paths through the grass, and the fountain."

"Is the fountain running?"

It isn't running, it isn't even filled, but I think it would be better if it was.

"It is running! Look at that."

"I remember when we used to throw pennies in there when you were little."

The light changes, and we start moving again.

"I'm going to drive around the square and then loop back around here and head down the rest of the way."

"Sounds good, sounds good."

"I'm passing the front of the square now, to our left. That old cannon is still here."

"Do you see anyone throwing pennies into the fountain?"

"I do! There's a little girl in a pink and white dress, standing near her father. He's handing her pennies and she's throwing them in."

I don't see this, of course—the fountain is still, cold, barren. I wonder when it last held water, if it's been long.

"Just like you did!" Dad beams. His smile is my reward for lying, for telling him things that aren't really there.

"And now we're passing by the big white church, it's on your right, and there's a large group just exiting the front doors. It looks like a receiving line for a wedding!"

"Well, isn't that something!"

I can see that it's a funeral, not a wedding. There's a notice on the bulletin board, and the small group that just exited is sad, dark, respectful.

"What a nice day for a wedding," Dad says.

I take a deep breath now, unsure of what I'm doing. I'm coming around the other side of the square, near where we started, but instead of moving into the lane that would take us down Main Street, I stay in the left turn lane and start another loop of the square. I need a few more seconds to think. Dad doesn't seem to notice that we're still moving in a circle. If he does notice, he doesn't say anything.

I make it around the square a second time, and we're out of the rotary and straightening onto the main thoroughfare. Now we're driving alongside the wide, tree-lined sidewalks that edge the storefronts. I note the brick façade of Susan's Verandah, a store my mom often visited, and I'm glad to see it's still here. There's a long, purple dress in the window. Mom would have loved it.

"Dad, here's the Verandah. Mom's favorite store. Remember?"

"I don't know how many hours she spent in that store."

"There's this long, purple dress in the window, and—"

"Your mother would have loved it," he finishes for me.

I'm realizing, quickly, how much has changed. The Verandah remains, but not much else looks familiar. Trudell's Pharmacy has closed, recently too, from the looks of it.

"Dad, here's Trudell's." I wait to see if he mentions them closing.

"Now there's a wonderful family business. I'm so happy to see them doing well."

And I leave it at that.

We're passing Joe's Pastry now, or what remains of it. The restaurant is gone, replaced by an insurance office. Joe's had been one of our family's favorite breakfast spots, and it's hard to imagine this downtown without them. I'm worried that if I lie about Joe's, Dad will want to stop in for a donut. I don't know what to tell him.

And that upscale restaurant, Peter James, the one where Paul Newman ate when he came to town, is a pizza place.

And The Melody Shop, the music store where Dad used to work, is a Thai restaurant.

And that jewelry store, the one where Dad bought Mom her diamond earrings, is a children's boutique.

We're driving in silence now. Dad sits quietly next to me while I find a place to turn around. Even the traffic patterns have changed, and soon I'm in another small rotary, looping around, and heading back up towards the square.

I have to say something, so I lie again.

"Sorry about that. I was going too fast to see everything. Let's drive down again."

"That's okay," he tells me. "I remember what it looks like."

His face is turned out the window, remembering the old

places we loved.

We're nearing the square again, but I spot an empty parking space and steer into it. I turn off the car and start rummaging through my pile of change.

"How would you feel about throwing some pennies?" I ask him, and he grins, and while we're walking to the square his hand is in mine, and we're back in that time, before, when pennies always found water.

Parenthood
Marina White

"Yes *please*, Mason," I said to my four-year-old as he chanted my name impatiently waiting for his fish sticks. Parenthood is so unforgiving at times. I wondered if he'd ever learn his manners or if he'd be eighteen years old and still using his sleeve as a napkin . . . Or worse yet, *my* sleeve as one.

"Mason I'm not your servant. I'm your mother. It makes me feel bad when you don't ask me nicely for things."

"What's a *servant*, Mummy?" I often forget I'm talking to a kid who hasn't learned such words.

"A servant is someone who—" He had already moved on to his toy fire truck making the noise of a siren as if there was some emergency he had to take care of. I thought of his father, managing some crisis of his own somewhere. I wanted Mason to understand and listen to me so badly it hurt sometimes. I wanted him to learn so that we could talk more. I wanted my life back, instead of centered on him, taking an hour and a half to get through lunch and move on. I cursed myself for even thinking that. How could I hate the nature of a four-year-old? I put his fish sticks on his plate and sat down to my own. He stopped playing with his truck and looked at the food.

"Thanks, Mummy. You're the best." He smiled at me and then picked up a fish stick and stuck in his mouth. He didn't realize what he'd just done. But it meant the whole world to me. Yes, parenthood was an uphill battle. Yes, I would get frustrated and think that he wasn't learning. But it was moments like these that made me thank God for the gift he'd given me. Parenthood, I realized, was the most rewarding job a person could ever have. "Can we go to Jake's house after lunch Mum, can we?" I smiled. Right now, I'd give him the whole world if he asked for it.

"I'll call Jake's mom and see if Jake can play today, okay?" He smiled his crooked smile at me and showed me how his firefighter was rescuing a cat from a tree that was about to fall. And I watched and I listened as if there was nothing else going on around me . . . Because at that moment, that's what it felt like.

Recognition
Scott M. Baker

Awareness came suddenly. One moment its world was dark and without sensation. The next, it opened its eyes and stared into the sky. It squinted against the sudden brightness. Several seconds passed before its eyes grew accustomed to the glaring light; however, it could still not make out its surroundings because a murky film covered the irises, casting the world into a blur.

As it lay on the ground, it tried to remember who it once was and how it had gotten here. The memories were there, lodged in the recesses of its mind, but buried so deep they seemed fleeting images. It experienced consciousness, but no complex thoughts or emotions. It could not even recall its own name, or if it even had one. All it could remember was a deep-rooted terror that lingered in its subconscious, though of what it could not recall.

Something moved in its peripheral vision. A woman stumbled by a few feet distant. It tried to make out her features, but she appeared only as a cloudy image. It recognized other figures nearby, each shuffling along. Instinctively, it felt danger and cried out. No words came, only a belabored moan. The others replied in kind, but none of them made threatening moves. Whatever they were, they didn't pose a threat.

It tried to stand, but nothing happened. Slowly, as it remembered how to work its muscles, its arms lifted off the ground and its legs kicked. With considerable effort, it rolled onto its stomach and struggled to its feet, its limbs not responding the way it wanted. Its right arm slipped as it pushed itself up. Falling face first onto the pavement, it felt its nose break and several teeth dislodge. An inner consciousness told it there should be pain, but there was none. It tried again, this time moving slowly and carefully, pushing itself into a kneeling position. With great effort, it stood, although the cumbersome legs made the task difficult. It nearly toppled over, reaching out at the last second to catch itself on a nearby police barricade covered in barbed wire. A strange sensation tore along the palm of its hand, but it ignored the feeling. It got to its feet and stood erect, wobbling for several seconds as its legs threatened to collapse, until finally it found its footing.

Raising its hand, it stared at where the barbed wire had ripped across its palm. The metal left a deep gash from the forefinger to the wrist that exposed the muscles. A reddish-brown liquid seeped from the opening. It flexed its fingers. The wound spread apart, revealing the bone underneath and forcing more of the ooze into its palm. Again, something in its subconscious told it that this should hurt, yet it felt nothing.

Agony tore through its body. Not from where it had cracked its face onto the pavement or from the gash in its hand, but from the pit of its stomach. Its vision blurred. Its legs grew numb, and its arms trembled. Doubling over, it clutched its abdomen as an insatiable hunger ravaged its insides. It desperately needed to feed. But on what? Despite all efforts, it could not remember what it ate. It let out an anguished howl, as much from pain as frustration. The others around it stopped and bellowed back in an inhuman chorus.

As suddenly as the hunger had started it stopped, or rather devolved into a dull ache that churned inside its stomach. What few senses remained slowly returned. It had no idea what to do next. Looking from side to side, it sought guidance from those around it. The others resumed walking, though it had no idea where they were going. For some unknown reason, it felt the need to follow. It took its first uncertain step and began to topple over. Jerking back, it barely stopped itself from falling. Slowly, the primordial brain grew accustomed to basic motor control. As it became more familiar with its legs, it staggered along in the general direction of those around it.

The disorientation remained, however. It had no idea where it was heading or why the others wandered in this direction. After a few yards, it bumped into the door of an abandoned police car. For a moment it continued to walk, pushing against the exterior, but got nowhere. A grunt escaped from its throat. As it flung itself to the right, the path became unobstructed, allowing it to continue on its way.

Ahead, light glimmered off the surface of a nearby building. Maybe the light was food? Its stomach ached in anticipation. More certain of its footing now, it quickened its pace and headed for the glimmer, hoping to find something to satiate the hunger.

As it approached the building, it caught sight of its reflection in the plate glass window and stared. It wore a white shirt and brown sports coat, both of which were stained with gore. The left side of its neck and half its face had been chewed off, leaving gnawed flesh that still glistened with blood, and exposing the spine and jaw. As it opened and closed its mouth, the image in the glass did the same. Was that what it really looked like? Reaching up, it stuck its fingers into the neck wound and felt around. The skin and muscles felt wet. It reached in deeper and caressed its spine, amazed by the texture of the bone.

A memory pushed into its consciousness. It remembered being attacked by things similar to itself, of fighting them off, of being dragged to the ground and ravaged. It had a brief recollection of overwhelming terror, though it could no longer comprehend what that emotion meant or what caused it. It recalled an intense, overriding pain. As the synapses of its brain fired off, it recounted those final moments before becoming one of the living dead.

"Daddy!"

It looked around, trying to find where the sound came from.

"Daddy! You're alive!"

The shout came from behind. Lumbering around to look in that direction, it saw a little girl about ten years old running toward it, her arms outstretched. A woman in long blonde hair chased after her, screaming for the girl to stop. A spark of acknowledgment fired off deep in its brain. It recognized the little girl. Stumbling forward, it went to meet the approaching child.

The noise had attracted the attention of the others. The collective moaning grew frantic as they turned toward the commotion and staggered toward the two humans. An emotion washed over it that its living form would have recognized as anger. It could not let them get to the child first. It had to reach the little girl before the others.

Pushing forward, it stumbled as fast as it could toward the girl, but several of the others were closing in. It growled a warning that went unheeded. They surrounded the child. Being small, she ducked under their outstretched arms and raced past them. Not so the woman. She tried to push her way through to reach her daughter, but they fell upon her and dragged her to the ground. Her screams echoed off the buildings. If any of them heard her, they didn't care. Hands clutched at the woman, ripping her clothes to reveal skin or tearing into her abdomen. As some of the others pulled out her intestines and began to eat, several dropped to their knees and chewed on the exposed flesh of her arms and legs. Her anguished cries eventually died out, replaced by the chomping of the others feeding off the body.

It ignored them, grateful for the distraction the woman created. It focused on the little girl, who raced toward it. As she got close, it dropped to its knees and stretched out its arms. The little girl ran into it and threw her arms around its neck. "I knew you'd be all right."

Its arms wrapped around the child, embracing her and holding her tight. Its mouth fell open and its lips curled back over its teeth. It recognized the little girl.

She was food.

St. Germaine and Blinking Colored Lights
An Excerpt
Kelly Dalke

I looked up from the bar and over at Jean, standing by the tree. Red, green, and yellow flashed across her face from the blinking lights. Her blonde hair was resting on her shoulders, and I could see the outline of her athletic body through her silk blouse. I refocused and carried the drinks I made over to the coffee table by the fire.

"Where is the little guy tonight?" I said to Laura, and then attempted to shove an entire scallop in my mouth, dripping grease from the bacon onto my sweater that blended into the tan wool.

"He's with Laura's mother," Gus replied. "I'll tell you what, that woman is horrible to be around, but man is it convenient having her so close by for babysitting."

"Gus, I would really appreciate it if you didn't talk about her that way. She's still my mother you know, and she does a lot for us, helping with Eli and everything."

"I know. That's what I was saying." Gus talked to Laura like he was a step ahead. He talked to everybody like that, always pretending to know better.

"Excuse me," said Laura, "I just have to check on dinner. It should be ready soon." She left us in the living room and went back into the kitchen.

"So Harrison, tell me about this latest exhibit you have going on," Gus said. He leaned back into the plush blue couch and sipped his cocktail.

"Well, it's a project I have been working on for the past few years, and I think I finally have enough to put a show together."

"It's amazing!" said Jean. "Really, the eye Harrison has

blows my mind with every new image. Especially with this project, he really had to look into people deeply to get what he needed."

"Thanks, honey, but I wouldn't go that far just yet. It still needs to be approved by the curator," I said. "I've always thought it was easier to see things for what they were when I had a lens in between me and my subject."

"It will," Jean said confidently. She put her hand on my thigh and smiled.

"Well, what is it about? What's the theme?" Gus asked. He always took it upon himself to get involved in my work. Constantly trying to give me advice on how to market myself to make a good profit. Gus was a successful financial planner and he thought he knew how to make everyone their maximum income. Laura entered the living room.

She said, "Let's continue this conversation in the dining room. Dinner is ready, and Harrison, I want to hear all about it. So come. Sit."

We grabbed our drinks and moved from the warmth of the fire to the formal dining room. Laura loved to entertain. I remembered when they were looking at houses, she made us come look at her final picks to give our opinion on which one we would like to have dinner. Jean and I told her it didn't matter to us, but she would say that it mattered to her. I voted on this one because of the location. It was easy for us to get to. We took our seats around the oval oak table. It was set like a photo from a Martha Stewart magazine. The different sized forks were perfectly placed. There were even burgundy cloth napkins folded in triangles on our gold-rimmed plates.

"So Harrison, tell us," Gus said.

"Okay, just keep an opened mind," I said.

"Jesus Harrison, just say it already," Gus said.

"The theme is . . . true happiness," I said, and sipped my

drink. I looked around the table and waited for a reaction. Usually, when I told people about my project, they'd have something to say. Some said, "oh, that's nice," while others asked, "what *is* true happiness?" and I'd just smile and walk away. Without looking up from his plate, Gus let out a *hmm* and began digging into his mashed potatoes.

"Why happiness," said Laura. "What made you think of that as a project, and how exactly do you photograph that?"

"I guess it started when I became tired of depressing art. I mean, I get it, people are drawn to other people's tragedies. Sometimes they enjoy relating, making it feel like they are not alone in the world, but I wanted to do something different. I wanted to give people hope, I suppose. All the unhappy people I know seem to have given up. It's like they truly believe that happiness does not exist any longer than their recent one night stand. I wanted to prove that it does, that it's possible."

"Awe, isn't that sweet," said Gus. "Our own St. Nick here, bring cheer throughout the year."

"Stop it, Gus," said Laura. "I think it is nice Harrison, and you're right. There is so much depressing art out there. It will be nice to see something focused on the positive, as opposed to someone's tragic life."

"Thank you, Laura," I said. "I'm used to the cynicism Gus, that's the point of it all."

"Don't get me wrong, it's a nice idea. I'm not trying to make fun. I think it's great. People would buy that, hang it on their wall. It's genius, making people believe they are happy," Gus said, with a mouth full of food while he waved his fork around. "You might do really well at this show Harrison."

"That's not the point of this one," Jean chimed in. "This is different. It's something Harrison feels strongly about, and he did it more for the sake of humanity than the money."

"You're still trying to sell though, right?" Gus stopped eating and awaited my response. His plaid oxford shirt had a perfectly pressed collar that poked out of his navy blue cable knit sweater.

"Of course. I would love to sell some pieces, but I'd also be happy with just a good turnout at the show. I have a portfolio in the car. I'll go get it to show you some examples."

I left the table, grabbed my keys from my coat, and went out to the car. I popped the trunk, and in looking for my leather portfolio, I saw the bag—the Christmas present I told Jean I wouldn't look at. I thought about it and decided one little peek wouldn't hurt. I still had to get her something, and at least then I'd have a gauge. I never knew what to get her. So I opened the bag using one finger, like it wouldn't be as obvious if I looked using less movement. There it was, a beautiful brown leather camera strap, looked like it even had my initials engraved on it, something I hadn't even mentioned or thought of. I grabbed my portfolio and put the bag back as it was.

When I came back in, Christmas music was softly playing from the stereo. Laura looked as if the effects of her third drink had begun to take place as she swayed to Judy Garland. She was an average sized woman, but such a lightweight and always the first to get drunk. When we would all go out together the night typically ended with Gus having to take her home.

"What's the difference between people in a happy moment and true happiness?" said Gus. He got up and grabbed a bottle of Gin and filled our glasses. Laura extended hers out to Gus and leaned into the table like she was still interested in the conversation but was really just trying to regain her balance.

"First, I observed people, their body language, and the

look in their eyes. Then, when I approached them about the project, I asked them a few questions. I guess I just had to read them and decide for myself."

"You must think you are a good judge of people to take on a project like that," said Gus.

"Yes, I do," I said. I opened the black leather book.

"Okay, so here is a couple I saw walking through the park. They had to be what, mid-'70s? They were touching the whole time. He either had his hand on her back, or she would grab his arm. They were inseparable." The photo I showed them was from a distance. The couple was sitting on a park bench in the far right of the frame. She sat with her head on his shoulder as they stared out at the swan boats floating across the pond. The opposing page in my book was another photo of the same couple, but a portrait. The happy lines on their faces were perfectly shadowed in black and white. I looked up at my friends. The girls were smiling, and Gus looked skeptical.

"These are great Harrison, really, but obviously a couple this age who is still together are most likely pretty happy," said Gus. "What about your average thirty-something waitress, or executive even. What about the guys paving the road the next block over? Did you get any from people like that?"

"Gus," Laura said.

"It's okay, Laura. I do have some like that Gus. Here, I'll show you the one I got while I was over by Hyde Park."

"What were you doing over there?" said Laura. "Please don't tell me you were walking around with your nice camera asking people if they were happy in that neighborhood."

I laughed. "It's not that bad," I said. Laura and Gus didn't know I grew up there, that it was here in their neighborhood I was most uncomfortable. I did almost get jumped that day, but thank God I was meeting an old friend who lived in the area. He showed up at the right time and has good face around there. He was a fellow artist who donated much of his time fixing up the neighborhood. He even placed some of his sculptures in a park. After the first one got stolen, the city let him cement them into the ground. I didn't tell Jean about it. I just turned the page of my portfolio instead.

"Here, this one is great. It's a woman alone with her son at the park. They were laughing while they ate fresh fruit she just bought from the outdoor market across the street. What I loved about her was how she was spending time with her son. She was really in the present with him. Not delegating, arguing, or pulling him along on adult business that he didn't want to go do. Most of the parents I see behave that way. Too busy to simply enjoy the time they have with their families."

I pointed out the way the soft evening sun created a glow around her hair while her head was back in laughter. Laura pointed out that her son's smile was infectious. I showed them a few more. A businessman who stopped to buy flowers for someone. A man playing music in the subway. I explained that what all these people had in common was a look in their eyes. It was a warm, calm, inviting look that I interpreted as happiness.

"An angry or unhappy person could not make someone feel this way," I said.

"These are great Harrison, beautiful pictures," Gus said. He topped off our drinks another time, and I could see he still wanted to say something. "But, I guess I still don't think that something like happiness is a long-term thing." He turned to me while holding the bottle. "So are you happy? Would you say you are one of these people?"

"Yes, I would." I looked over at my wife. She slightly smiled and looked back to Gus. While I looked at her, I couldn't help but think that there was something about that smile, but I felt as if it was my guilt, looking at the present that made me feel that way. She sipped her drink without looking at me.

"Okay then, fine, if you are going to be stubborn about it, we'll believe you are indeed completely happy, for the sake of the argument." Gus pushed his plate forward, with all but chicken bones, and broccoli stems left.

"Who's arguing here?" I said, "All I was doing was telling you about my project. You asked, and you don't have to believe in it either."

"Are you saying that you are not happy?" Laura said. Her glass slipped from her hand and smashed all over the rose-colored tiled floor. The glass and ice cubes glistened in the soft light.

"Okay, that's enough now," Jean said. She got up to get the broom. "Why don't you sit down, Laura, while I clean this up."

"That's not what I am saying at all. I am just saying that I think happiness is something that happens in moments. This dinner made me happy, this company makes me happy. Would I say that it's all I need? No. It's a natural thing to look one day ahead, and people do that to find more happiness. Do you think people go to work because they are already happy? No, they go to work to pay for the house that holds their family, and they take them closer to their goals. And that never ends, for anyone." Gus stood up and cleared his plate. I could tell the alcohol was fueling his enthusiasm.

"Well, I guess that's where we disagree," I added. Laura walked over to the radio turning up Bing Crosby's rendition of White Christmas, like she could care less about the conversation. "And I think you are missing my point. All I am trying to say is that it is possible to get yourself to a state of mind where you are just happy. That's all. Where your past doesn't matter, and the future is only a continuation of the life you are loving to live. There are people out there that have found that, and all I wanted to do is bring it to light." I walked over to him and put my hand on his shoulder.

Laura abruptly turned to us and said, "Are you going to the parade, Jean?" She had a sparkle of carbonation in her eyes as she swayed to the music and turned back to the stereo. One of the black straps of her dress was starting to hang off her shoulder, and her hair was coming undone.

"Um, I haven't decided yet. Harrison, what do you think? Parade tomorrow?" Jean said to me. She was trying to wipe up the splatter of gin on the floor and had to move in and around Laura who refused to sit down.

"Sure, I love the parade," I said. I held in a laugh and Jean knew. She wasn't happy about it but I didn't care, it wasn't our story. "I guess we aren't making it to dessert," I whispered to her.

Perking up, Laura swung around. "I have a great idea," she said. She left the dining room and came back with what looked like a photo album. "Let's look at some old photos! I haven't done this in years." She put the old brown album on the table roughly, like it jumped out of her hands.

"Oh, good idea Laura," said Jean. We gathered around the table again. Gus was looking at his phone. I almost brought up the idea of being present again but decided to leave it alone.

"Wow. Look at that hair! I hope people that smoked steered clear of me," said Jean. "Seriously, there is enough aqua net in there to ignite like gunpowder!"

"Well at least you stayed away from the blue eyeliner," Laura said, and she flipped the pages. I looked at the next photo of Jean. It was taken around the time we met. She looked so beautiful. The picture was of her, Laura, and a couple of other friends. Her smile in the photo belonged in my show. It was real, genuine, and happy. It looked, different.

Gus grabbed the bottle and went to fill our drinks another time. "Oh, no thank you Gus, one more of those and I will be on the floor with your glassware," Jean said.

"Harry, I know you are still good for one more, we are celebrating after all." He topped off my glass and raised his. He only calls me Harry when he is drunk.

"To Harry! Making the world a happier place!" He shouted with his glass in the air. I clinked my glass to his, and as I went to sip it, he stopped me by putting his hand over the top.

"So, I *am* cynical. I am not one of the people in your show. But go ahead and take my picture, Harry. Put my smiling face in your show. I bet nobody would even know the difference."

We all just sat there looking at our drinks. The sound of I'll be home for Christmas was softly flowing out of the stereo, and the blinking lights continued to change the colors of the room.

Blue-Collar Father
An Excerpt
Nolan R. O'Connell

Some nights it's 4:30, some nights it's 6:00. When his son was younger, Dan wouldn't get home at night sometimes until 8:00 to pat his boy on the head and nuke the dinner plate his wife, Julie, had prepared for him. Regardless of the time he comes home, Daniel is tired. He's *tired*. He wobbles on what seems like half broken knees to his desk where he takes his things out of his lunchbox, finishes his cigarette, and then painfully gets up to stand and walks to the bathroom. He makes his way back to his desk where he will check his e-mail and updates on all his favorite websites. He might peruse through Yahoo! For a while to see what the leaders of the world are doing to ruin it outside of his small suburb. His wife cooks him dinner and he eats, and at 7:30 switches to his recliner and Julie lays on the couch. Somewhere he will take a shower and pick the metal chips from his hair and wipe the grime from his fingernails. Nights end early because his day starts early, so he goes to bed. The bed is a vessel for a restless night's sleep full of still pain in his joints after standing on concrete in steel-toe boots all day. When he finally falls asleep, only a few hours later he will wake up and make the same commute and work the same workday. He does this seven days a week, every week, to put his boy through college.

I was thirteen at the time and had little experience with death, but I remember this moment well because of the look on my father's face when he found it. We walked into my grandfather's garage, a place I was very partial to in my youth and still am today. It smelled like grease and woodstove and held every tool known to man on its walls or in aluminum toolboxes. Pulleys hung from the grates in the ceiling that could hoist an entire vehicle clear off the ground. Naked women on calendars decorated the refrigerators and murals of the Rial Side Knights hung above the workbenches. My father walked through the door in the garage door as I followed, and no one was in there, which was unusual because usually everyone was in there laughing and drinking, but instead they were inside the house on the hill where my father grew up in doing the same. He found an old toolbox, possibly the oldest one in the garage, and started to open the drawers. Clearly, he was looking for something my grandfather had kept. He finally came to the last drawer, and he found it there lying about other tools like it had been thrown there carelessly one day. He picked it up with both hands, head facing upward, and looked downward at me and said "Thor," It was partially rusted and the grip had hardened grease on it. It had dents in the head and scratches down the handle. He gripped it with one hand, and the light from the handle glistened in his eyes and in mine.

His wife was a blind date. He had been on many dates as his roommate's wingman, and he didn't care that this would be any different. The first time they met, Dan had greasy black hair and a bandana. He burnt Julie's dress with a cigarette and she hated him for it too. Either he has a certain charm in his character, or she saw the genuine man he truly was. Though he never asked her to, later in life, when he left on long trips swordfishing and trawling she waited for him. When he went out one day and called from Virginia to tell Julie he had joined the United States Coast Guard, she waited for him. Years later when he was laid off from his job, and laid off again, and again, she waited still. Now as he sits in his chair in the living room, Dan occasionally looks over to the couch where Julie lays in her pink robe snoring over the volume of the television, he remembers the girl whose dress he burned and how much he loves her for staying.

Dan's been a lot of things over the span of his life. From mixing and laying cement to carving metal away with a machine. He was in a band, he owned his own auto repair business, and he was a fisherman. Fishing swordfish was the job he found the most joy in. "There's nothing like hauling in a line and having a nine-hundred to twelve-hundred-pound swordfish on the end of it thrashing away," he would say, remembering the days out on the water. He caught a lot of sharks too as they would come up to get bait or chum. Sometimes he'd throw the chum over the stern to watch the sharks follow the boat, eagerly trying to get every last piece. Lobster trapping was a lot of fun too, but harder work. Fishing was a lot of fun for him, but nothing he would want to do forever.

He's a machinist. Machining is what he does. He does it because he can take a piece of metal, like a round piece of raw stock and make something that gets sent into space for satellites and space shuttles. He made pieces for one of the Mars rovers and pieces for the Hubble telescope. He's made parts for hospital equipment too. He loves making this material and was once interested in what he was doing his work for. After doing his trade for so long, the purpose of the job doesn't matter as much, "You just want to make the parts," he says. There's a pride he gains in carving something from a piece of material, so that's his trade. he presses a combination of buttons that move the drills into place and carve chunks of material away until a complex chunk of angles, edges, and holes is left. He's the best at his trade, the man everyone goes to when they mess up a part and need to save their asses. He can fix anything and knows how to run every one of the monstrous, one-ton machines. One time many years ago, he cut his hand wide open on one of these machines and went to work the next day to finish his job. He has piles upon piles of metal drill bits in the drawers of his toolboxes with pictures of his family taped to the box.

Now, Daniel O'Connell sits on a beach in southern New Hampshire in tranquility, surrounded by tall pine, birch, and oak trees. The sun sets in front of him as fish make ripples in the calm, flat lake as they approach the surface to feed and sometimes jump. His son fishes late on the dock in front of him, swatting the mosquitos from his arms, and looking up toward the skies for distant worlds. Tomorrow he'll have to work on the car's engine in the quiet of midday while bird's chirp around him and maybe a visiting neighbor will stop by. But for tonight, he'll lie in bed at night next to Julie thinking to himself, while outside the peepers are peeping and an owl may occasionally hoot, about his life and the ones he loves. There's not too much that can disturb him greatly and there's even less that can upset him too much. He has his family and his home and his son is growing successful and that's all that will matter to him for the rest of his life.

"I got no regrets. I've got a great son, makes me proud on a daily basis, I've got a decent job that I like, I'm comfortable now where I live, you know? It's not bad. I'm not in the best of places, but I'm not in the worst. I'm happy where I am right now." —Daniel O'Connell

11.2.16
Stacy Hannings

I overheard a conversation the other day, and I can't stop thinking about it. Maybe if I write it down, I can make some sense of what I heard.

I had gone into a fitting room with an armload of things, hoping to find a few last-minute scores before I set off on my winter adventures. Nothing was fitting right, and I was feeling discouraged. My tan I worked at all summer long seemed to have vanished overnight, and the one dress I did like wasn't on clearance. I had struck out. Oh well.

As I was gathering my things I heard a teenage sounding girl latch the door next to me and call out, "I'll just be a sec, Dad!" I put my boots on and sat down to tie them up, regretting the decision to wear shoes that needed lacing. I can hear the sighs from the girl next to me as she fiddles with hangers. Her dad calls out, "Any luck?"

She responds, "No, nothing fits! Ugh! My body is terrible."

My body is terrible.

That's really what she said.

Her dad said nothing.

I said nothing.

Why didn't either of us say anything?!

That's really what's eating me up about this.

Why didn't I call through the wall between us?

"Your body is not terrible, not even a little bit. It's the cookie cutter department store clothing that's terrible. It's the media infecting young girls (and boys) that's terrible. It's labels like 'one size fits all,' or my personal favorite—'one size fits most'—that are terrible. It's XL women's clothes being S men's clothes. It's being a size 10 in one store and a size 18 in another. It's the plus-size models that are hardly plus-sized. It's movies and music and a whole culture focused on skinny. It's our self-worth being so wrapped up in how well clothes fit us that is terrible. But not your body. Your body is yours, and it's perfect for you."

I didn't say any of that.

And I hate that she probably went home that day and didn't hear anything to change her mind.

But I do get it. I so get it.

I can't speak for anyone but myself, and my own teenage brain probably thought the same things. In middle school and high school, I was consumed by insecurities. I always felt like I was the biggest girl among my friends, my class, my team. It didn't matter the group, I always compared myself. Gosh, I look back at photos now and realize how horribly skewed my thoughts were. Stacy, you were just tall. Why did you waste so much time thinking you were fat?

It wasn't until college that I began to realize how much better I felt when I stopped obsessing over my body. I stopped caring about the clothes I wore and just put on whatever felt comfortable. Yeah, so what none of it matches and I may have slept in it last night, I feel like myself. And you know what? I like myself.

I've always hated those lofty blanket statements like "love yourself" or "love the skin you're in." Everyone's relationship with their own body is completely unique, and who am I to tell you how you should feel or how you should act? My motto would be something more along the lines of "Every day, try to make your body your own." Just try. It's okay if you can't. And every day, because every day is different. Some days I feel like a complete stranger in my body, and other days I feel so perfectly fused with it that a smile feels most comfortable.

It still makes me sad that that girl in the fitting room felt so poorly about herself. I hope she had better luck elsewhere and found something that made her feel confident. I hope her dad told her she looked beautiful no matter what she wore.

I hope I say something next time.

But mostly, I hope there isn't a next time.

Fields of Forgotten Lessons
Elizabeth R. Jurgilewicz

My parents buried every animal we ever lost in our backyard. What started as a small garden of fanciful blooms turned into a long expanse of growth mere feet above layers of those we lost. As a child, I never quite understood why everyone felt so sad about this place. Why people would come and cry near a specific flower. Why I was not allowed to go there while others kneeled in sorrow.

My first memory of this place is coated in a swarth of warm, golden air. The sun casts no shadows, yet it sets around me. Everything is quiet, even the wind taking a moment to breathe and steady. I am standing on one of the large rocks encasing the normally solemn place. My bare feet steadily absorb the heat from below, my summer dress hanging loosely around tiny legs, while my hands grasp onto ends of long braids. The energy of the world around me ebbed away as I stepped off the tall stone I stood upon, landing heavily upon faded grass. To this day, I cannot quite grasp how the world shifted so quickly.

It was as if suddenly, with the sun disappearing under the tree line and the residual light still surrounding us, the world came alive for a moment more. The whole garden was a sea of daisies. No matter where I turned, hundreds were holding open, hearts towards the sky, taking in their final moments before rest. I walked slowly through this ocean of white and yellow, the wind starting again to create a tide of petals brushing against my arms and face. For the first time, I walked to the memorial flowers, ran my fingers along them, and closed my eyes to feel what those before had.

As I came towards the center, my height allowing only daisies to reach my eyes, the final seconds of light drifted away. The flowers began to close. I was left in the center of a graying, encased, static field. This is the moment I understood why I was not allowed here during times of grief. This is the moment I felt loss for the first time. The moment my heart broke and my tiny knees touched the ground as cold air wrapped around me in a final farewell.

I was four years old when day turned to night and an endless field of daisies said goodbye. They would not reopen until the next summer, teaching me that seasons of life are meant to ebb and flow, not remain static in a memory of nostalgic bliss. I never quite understood this until I became an adult and saw how my parents missed the childhood I spent too quickly. I see my family now, all grown to a new beginning, and I feel the start of a season. Our field of daisies has begun to blossom, bringing another stage of warmth and life.

I will always miss the previous blooming moments. The moments of being a child in a world of memory, walking above those who made the growth above possible. I can still see the golden light which lacked shadows and feel the warmth seeping into the core of everything I had known before. The sun may have set, and the daisies may have fallen over years past, but with each beat of my heart, a new generation blooms before me. A new season. A new light. A new moment to someday remember. With this in mind, I walk along the daisies, feeling home wherever their petals sway.

How Horses Heal
Carter Saltmarsh

As dawn approaches, Jonathan tosses and turns when his six-fifteen alarm clock abruptly goes off and he lazily wipes the eyelashes from his tired eyes. A pile of clothes is neatly made by his dresser, and he scurries to the bathroom to start his day. The hot water from the shower helps him finally awaken from his sleep and quickly jumps out to put on his clothes. He combs his hair carefully and adds hair gel for the hair to stick nicely in one spot, then hurries down the stairs toward the kitchen. Jonathan's mother has already been awake and has made breakfast as Jonathan sits down to eat. She has placed his lunch neatly in a colorful lunch bag and then kisses him good morning as she turns on the television for the morning news. As the news starts to roll in, Jonathan runs back upstairs to brush his teeth and adds his lunch bag to his backpack full of homework. As he walks back down the stairs, his father greets him and gives Jonathan a hug and wishes him a good day. Jonathan's mother greets him at the door and gives Jonathon a kiss and tells him to learn something new with a smile. As he walks down the driveway, Jonathan turns; he smiles and waves to his parents who also wave in return and heads up the road to the school bus.

Jonathan was not your typical twelve-year-old sixth grader; he had a love of horses and was not afraid to show it. He had pictures of horses on his walls, dresser, and pillows, he wore sweaters with horses on them to school and even had a toy horse on his keychain. No one else in his family showed an interest in horses besides him, and he liked it that way. Jonathan made it to the bus stop and waited patiently in the warm spring New Hampshire sunshine. Minutes later, the other neighborhood kids started to arrive and also waited patiently for the bus. No one said hello or stood next to Jonathan; the other children seemed to ignore his presence and went on talking about their weekend, leaving Jonathan alone.

When the bus finally arrived and opened its doors, Jonathan nervously climbed the stairs, quickly found an available seat and sat down quietly. As the bus started to move, the neighboring kids next to Jonathan began to taunt him. They laughed at his sweater of a trotting Saddlebred that his grandmother had bought for him and snickered among another, spreading the word around the bus. Bravely, he ignored the commenting and began to read until the bus got to the school.

At school, Jonathan did not go to the Cafeteria like all the other sixth graders when they arrived in the morning, instead he went to his reading teacher's classroom and pulled out a book and became lost in a sea of pages. While his teacher graded papers, Jonathan contently read. He loved to read and loved how peaceful it seemed to make everything. Suddenly, the bell to start Monday morning rang and the students began to assemble to classrooms and staff hurried along the stragglers. Jonathan's classroom began to quickly fill with kids and his palms quickly became sweaty with nerves. But the day went on smoothly, better than Jonathan expected and he continued his day of learning. Everything was going good until right before lunchtime, when a boy named Adam approached Jonathan at his locker. "That lunch box is so gay!" "What are you a girl?" Adam laughed. Adam knocked Jonathan against the lockers and walked away with a bunch of students, laughing and whispering to each other so Jonathan couldn't hear. With a sick feeling in his stomach, Jonathan held back his tears, picked up his lunch box and headed to the library.

Jonathan sometimes went to the library to eat his lunch

because it was the only place where he could relax and eat his lunch contently without anyone making fun of him. He sat in the farthest corner of the library, pulled out a book on horses and began to read. He did not know why kids his age taunted him and bullied him because of what he wore or what he had for valuables, but Jonathan kept going throughout his day, knowing that everything was going to be fine. The last class of the day was gym, and Jonathan was actually athletic, so class did not bother him as much as others. Until he got to the locker room.

As he walked into the locker room, the other boys attacked him with hurtful comments. One boy giggled, "The girl's locker room is down the hall!" Another boy snarled "This is not a room for faggots" and pushed Jonathan aside. Everyone in the locker room began laughing and Jonathan walked out trembling with fear. This time it was a little too much and a tear streaked down his face. He wanted today to be over and could not wait until his mother picked him up after school. Jonathan looked forward to every afternoon after school because it only meant one thing: it was time for his riding lesson.

The barn where Jonathan took riding lessons was about thirty minutes from his house and either his mother or father drove him to his lessons every day. As the car turned from pavement to a long dusty driveway, Jonathan forgot about the tormenting from school and started to focus on his horse which he would be riding. His mother parked the car and the two of them walked into the barn where the horses were kept. The sweet smell of hay and the sound of horses snorting as they ate their afternoon grain gave Jonathan a smile as he passed the row of stalls. A long, black face with whiskers peered over a stall near the end of the barn and gently nickered as Jonathan approached and scratched the horse's velvety muzzle. Luke was the horse's name and he was always happy to see Jonathan. "I have something for you Luke," Jonathan explained. The boy pulled a carrot from his riding jacket pocket and held it out to Luke who gently grasped the carrot from Jonathan's palm and chewed the treat contently. "I'll be in the tack room Jonathan" his mother smiled and she walked down to speak with the riding instructor to announce their arrival.

Jonathan slipped Luke's halter on and carefully walked the old horse into the aisle way to be groomed and tacked up. Jonathan curried away dirt from Luke's back, then patted the old horse's neck and began talking to him about the horrible day he had. As Jonathan talked, Luke's ears constantly moved back and forth, listening to everything the boy had to say. When Jonathan was finished grooming the horse, he placed a saddle carefully on Luke's back and fastened the girth. With the saddle securely fastened, Jonathan slipped the bridle onto Luke's head, placed the metal bit into the horse's mouth and fastened the cheek pieces. Before the boy and horse entered the riding ring, Jonathan lovingly gave Luke a hug around the horses massive neck and thanked his mount for not only listening but also for being a friend to talk to and to have someone that does not judge you for what you wear or how you talk but being someone with a tremendous heart and having the amazing gift of learning to be yourself. With that, Jonathan and Luke went on to take many lessons together, won ribbons at horse shows, trail rides through the meadows and formed a friendship that made memories that Jonathan cherished forever. All because of a horse, Jonathan forgot about the bullying because a horse named Luke saved him.

The Last Lap
Stephanie Martin Glennon

It was an unspeakably awful thing to say.

After an exhausting and unnecessary verbal battle, the hospice's medical director—who had been openly skeptical of my physician husband's emphatic wish not to die in a hospital, when I was the one to press it—asked whether my husband wanted to drive home with me or whether he wanted an ambulance to take him.

The doctor added, out of my earshot but not that of our friend and my sisters-in-law, "You might as well, for your last lap."

This remark's casual cruelty—its trivialization of my husband's determination to come home, its grotesque appropriation of the fundamental unit of an unending journey, when we all knew this was a one-way trip to an imminent and shockingly early end of life—makes my heart race even now, as I sit alone in a different home in summer rain more than five years later.

One of the many privileges of parenthood has been getting to know my children's remarkable friends. Not long ago I went to a senior honors presentation by one of them, who gave a talk about linguistics and Jacques Lacan, and introduced me to a French Holocaust survivor's account of a uniquely healing moment.

Gérard Miller's film *"Rendez-vous chez Lacan"* shares her story of having been haunted for two decades by nightmares of the Gestapo seizing her and her family; she was describing a recent nightmare when Lacan leaped up and ran his hand along her face—converting the terrifying power of the word "Gestapo" into, in her native French, a tender touch, a *g'este à peau* that she was able to recall as a physical memory.

In the ambulance on the way home, I had clutched the neon pink card-stock portable DNR in my left hand, rolled like a diploma and splotched with my tears. I had touched my right hand to the side of my husband's unlined temple and cheek. A *g'este à peau*.

It's well past time for me to reclaim that journey home, our last trip together.

The ambulance arrived at the hospital late in late afternoon's high sun, an hour-and-a-half after we had been assured it would come.

We had a quiet ninety minutes with no one checking vital signs, trying to administer medication, or appearing awkwardly at the door. No machines buzzing or beeping. I had not realized how unaccustomed we were to being undisturbed.

The room's single window could not be opened, and the temperature seemed to rise at an unbearable rate. We lay together on the hospital bed.

Eventually growing restless, Jim mustered the energy to walk a single circle around the unit floor, leaning against me. This was the same hospital where he worked, and every physician and nurse and staff member who saw us looked at us somberly and silently, some of them wiping away tears.

Our children and friends had been at our house for hours, setting it up for Jim's return.

The ambulance's two-person crew appeared at the entrance to Jim's room as I gathered his things. By that time the things we carried were few. The driver seemed surprised to see me there.

"It's okay if I ride with you?" I asked.

"Yes, but you understand you have to ride in front. You can't be in the back."

"That's fine," I said.

I walked alongside the gurney and into the elevator, my hand on Jim's shoulder. We stepped out on the first floor, through a sequence of sets gently *whooshing* sliding doors, into intense sunlight. I squinted and turned away to see Jim's boss, our friend, speed-walking into the hospital just inches away, to a rare Friday evening meeting.

She immediately hugged me and I became undone, hysterically weeping into her shoulder, "He wants to go home and I just can't stand the thought . . ." I did not mean the thought of going home but of his dying. I simply could not believe that time had come. She held onto Jim and whispered to him.

The ambulance driver stood silently, and by the time Jim's boss had disengaged from both of us, looked at me— undoubtedly an immeasurably pitiful sight, weeping and holding that pink paper anyone in that line of work can identify—and said, "You can go in the back."

I sniffled into my sleeve. "No, that's okay, I can sit up front."

The crew looked at me and spoke in unison. "*Please* get in the back."

For the first among thousands of trips we had made together on the same road, we faced backwards, our view of the familiar obstructed only by the outlined letters spelling "Ambulance."

The siren was off.

Only afterwards did I begin to imagine, when seeing a silent ambulance, that it might contain someone truly on the way home.

Jim brought up two subjects, one wildly practical, and one from his heart.

His conversational palette cleanser was a ministerial reminder to me, from his cautiously frugal persona as the family financial planner who had in each child's infancy begun saving the college money that went on to be dissipated without him. He would not live to see any of his children graduate.

As the ambulance pulled out in front of the hospital building where Jim had been bombarded with fruitless chemotherapy and radiation, he said, "You need to remember to cancel my phone line, because it's a hundred dollars a month."

That out of the way, he paused and told me quietly, "It's important to do something for Bob." His physician partner. Our friend, who never left his side once we got home.

I would have to think about that for several weeks more.

Jim's last trip covered the same stretch of road we had traveled thousands of times, to and from Jim's work, our daughters' high school, and my work far away along the highway to which it connects.

We had turned left onto that road on the way to the hospital when I was in labor with our first child, then nicknamed "Bud," on an uncharacteristically cool August day.

We covered exactly the same route when Jim drove us from our first home to the hospital where our next three children were born. Each time, the return trip on this road was made with the newest addition swaddled in an oversized, grandmother-knit sweater—first white, then mint green, then yellow—slouched into a backward-facing infant seat. Summer, spring, and two winters.

The only other time I had been in an ambulance on this road, all of the children (then numbering three) had been with me. Jim had calmly been waiting in the emergency room on the other end: Noah, at two, had hit his head in a fall onto cement and had an ostrich egg-sized lump on his forehead. The ambulance crew gave him a green velveteen teddy bear, a gift that provided him comfort long afterwards.

Years ago, there had been two working dairy farms. The children never tired of exclaiming "Moo cows!" every single time they saw the rural wonder, any more than the beagles tire of the sound of the same food clattering like tiny pebbles into their metal bowls twice every day.

We passed the bakery where we had picked up treats for family celebrations and where on the way to preschool years earlier a well-weathered man had given our four-year-old daughter a two-dollar bill that he said had been passed along to him in a bakery for good luck when he was about her age.

"Has it worked for you?" I asked him.

"It has."

We passed the SPCA, where our younger daughter had fallen in love with countless animals and we had brought two of them home forever.

We passed the family farm stand where we had picked out juicy summer tomatoes, buttercup corn, fall pumpkins, and gourds . . .

We passed fairgrounds where we had gone every summer, one son somehow deftly outmaneuvering the games' designers so he could bring back arms full of enormous stuffed animals for his little sisters.

This was the same park where we had trudged through many annual fairs, including one only days before an August birth, when my feet were so swollen that I had to borrow huge tennis shoes from our visiting friend Jon's trunk. He took a look at me and laughed heartily, dubbing me "Preggo the Clown."

We had traveled that stretch of road at the beginning of nearly all our family vacations, loaded with sand toys and summer books—or ski equipment in a rack on top that I invariably forgot about before doing some degree of damage pulling into the garage at trip's end.

Almost every day our daughters spent at high school involved at least two nearly identical round-trips.

The road branched off at about the half-way point towards our dear friends' house, which had been the siren call to moving across the state line when Jim began practicing medicine two weeks before our first son was born.

Eventually, we had driven the same route between home and the hospital to get Jim to the Emergency Room for a sequence of horrific complications. It was always in a blizzard.

This time we pulled into our driveway just in front of a van bearing bright spring tulips from a cousin in California. Our friends and family were there to meet Jim. He declined the stretcher and walked inside on his own steam. He never suffered again.

The ambulance pulled away.

Inside our home, until he peacefully lost consciousness less than a day before he died, Jim laughed with friends among endless tender words and gestures.

"At last I was sure
That you weren't far away from home."

Benedictine and Me
Nicole Turner

My childhood was filled with grass stains and imaginary wonders. Most of my memories were made alongside my best friend, Lizzie. Looking back, it makes sense that she was the one who first brought me to Benedictine Park. Her childhood was also filled with grass stains and imaginary wonders, maybe even more so than mine. It was a perfect summer day between the third and fourth grade. Her dad packed sandwiches in plastic baggies and lemonades in glass jars, and the three of us piled into their silver minivan. We pulled off of the main road and into the dirt lot, empty but for two cars. Lizzie and I jumped out as soon as the car was in park and ran ahead of her dad, who followed with the food. We stopped at a wooden sign that described the history of the park behind foggy plexiglass. Lizzie told me that her dad had something to do with working in the park and he instantly seemed like a god.

We walked past the wall of trees that separated the parking lot from the fields themselves and found ourselves among rolling green hills. Lizzie and her dad knew exactly where to go and soon we were halfway between a tree, with leaves of a purple hue, and the top of the biggest hill. We laid a blanket down and set up the food. At some point, we ate the sandwiches and drank the lemonade, but all I remember is exploring the vast grounds surrounded by promising forest. Lizzie was eager to show me her favorite spots, not knowing that they would soon become mine as well. We raced down the hill towards the purple tree, which shaded a cool stone bench. It looked like the perfect tree to climb, but our excitement didn't give us the patience for that. We darted through a gap in the hedges that ran beside the tree, and I felt as though I had entered into a magical land. There were walls of hedges on either side of us, creating an aisle that led to a circle of trees. It became our palace. The circle of trees was our throne room, with the large stone in the middle acting as an elegant throne. Gaps in the hedges led us into alcoves among the limbs, and soon our imaginations were crafting rooms, our young minds ignoring the crushed beer cans that littered the forest floor alongside pine needles. One of the last gaps we found led to the biggest opening and our favorite spot. It was large enough that we could climb the branches that constructed the hedge while still being concealed by its leaves. When we stood by the purple tree and looked at the outside of this hedge, our imaginative eyes saw a face—the face of a monster. We made up a game where one of us would go inside the hedge and manipulate the branches to make the mouth and eyes move. We would tell stories to each other through the monster's mouth. Often, the monster was a creature to be defeated, and we would imagine grand swords in our small hands, allowing us to ward off the evil.

We went back many times throughout our childhoods. We fought the monster and played in the hedges. We met a beautiful dog with pure white fur, which we began to see almost every time we went to the fields. We explored the lower hills and found an abandoned chicken coup in the woods, the eeriness of the decrepit shack striking fear within us. We would run to the very top of the tallest hill and roll all the way down, screams and laughter coming out intermingled, before standing up on wobbly legs to find red rashes blossoming on our skin from the rough grass. In the winter, we would sled down the same tall hill, finding ourselves weary and out of breath from trudging through the snow each time we had to make it back to the top. We felt as though we had found a magical land, like the ones we read of in books, our own Narnia or Terabithia.

We continued to go there as we entered the fifth grade. We extended our reach of exploration into a small forest between the fields and the road. There was a magnificently large tree there and we would spend hours climbing up it, sap sticking to our fingers. It felt like time stopped there. It was just us and our determination to climb to the top of the tree. Halfway up the maze of branches, we found a wooden platform tucked into the branches and nailed down. Once again, our young minds saw this as a magical discovery, part of a fortress, not noting the crumbling black burns all over it. To kill the time while climbing, we would play "would you rather," and force each other to choose between living with our evil gym teacher for a day or eating worms. We would always pick the worms.

Much later, sometime in middle school, I went there with my dad for an afternoon. I had gone with both of my parents once before to try geocaching and I remember it being an afternoon of fun. But this was after my parents had separated, and Thursdays were my day to see my dad. On this Thursday, we parked in the dirt lot and I ran to the purple tree. I wanted to show my dad how far up I could climb. I sat perched as far as I dared to go, looking out at the green fields while the wind blew in my hair. I could see people walking their dogs and others flying kites. I wondered why I always seemed to forget my kite. The bark was rough against my bare legs and my hair tangled in the branches, but I never felt more comfortable than I did there. Someone called me. I looked down to see a police officer standing at the base of the tree, looking up at me through dark sunglasses. He asked me what I was doing, and I stated simply that I was climbing the tree. My dad hurried over to see what was going on, telling me to climb down. I suppose the officer then realized how young I was because he apologized for the confusion and explained that high schoolers would often sit in the tree to do drugs, so he had to check. They talked casually for a bit before the officer left. I decided to climb back up the tree, challenging myself to go faster than I had the first time. I looked out again, seeing the fields I had known to be innocent.

I went less often after that, at least until high school. Sophomore year, my friend Iris and I decided to have a picnic at Benedictine to catch up after her annual month-long absence from town. We made food at our own houses and met at the park, embracing in a tight hug. She laid out a blue floral tablecloth and we placed down the food. She told me about her summer camp and her family vacation to Martha's Vineyard as we ate vegan chocolate chip cookies and sipped lemonade and seltzer. Ants climbed across the tablecloth to find remnants of the sweetness we were consuming. I had brought my Polaroid camera and we took pictures of us sitting on the grass and hanging from the branches of the purple tree. She took a Polaroid of me and gave me one of her. To take to college with us, she said, although we still had two full years left. I left the park that day with a full heart and the intention to come back.

Early in junior year, I went to Benedictine with the guy I liked, but who had liked my best friend. He brought his guitar and played music, and I listened in my floral sundress. He told me he didn't like my best friend anymore, that he liked me and wanted to go out with me. I began to feel very sick, although I'm sure it had nothing to do with him. My vision was coming in and out, shifting from the brightness of the sun to sudden blackness. He had to guide me carefully down the hill, stopping to let me take breaks when I became too dizzy. We waited until I felt better and then drove our respective ways home.

Eventually, we went on a real date. My first date, made

complete with flowers and dinner. We ended it at Benedictine. We placed a blanket on the side of the big hill and sat beneath the stars. The park felt different than it did when I was younger. With age, I had grown further from my fantasy and deeper into reality. I was still happy, only now it was happiness fostered from what was happening in my real life, rather than within my imagination. We talked for hours and pointed out constellations and talked about seeing the world. He asked if he could kiss me. I said yes. And I had my first kiss upon those hills. It wasn't how I thought it would be. We walked hand in hand back to his car and he kissed me again and we drove out of the dirt lot.

We went back once more while we were together, this time with three friends. Instead, on this particular night, we brought sleeping bags and cameras to the hillside. The fields were covered with people taking advantage of the open sky to view the red moon. Professional photographers had large cameras set up at the top of the hill. We were all bundled in our blankets and layers, talking and waiting for the lunar event. My friend teased the boy for putting his arm around me. We took many pictures, but our small camera phones struggled to capture the moon properly.

He and I did not last long. Later in that year, he ended up dating another one of my close friends. The three of us were driving around town one night and he decided that we should pick up his best friend and go to Benedictine. He wanted to set me up with him. I didn't think I wanted that, but I agreed anyway. The four of us sat on an uncomfortably small blanket. I was across from the boy who had given me my first kiss in this same spot, but now his arm was around my friend, and I was sitting next to his friend, expectations creating tension between us. I downloaded a constellation app onto my phone and kept my eyes on the map of stars.

Iris and I went back again in the summer before we started

college. We bought cookie dough and ice cream and sat on the blue floral tablecloth again. Iris had been away again for her annual summer activities, so we caught each other up on what we had been doing while we watched the sun set behind the trees. She had a new polaroid camera with her and said we could use the whole pack of film. So we did. We spent time dividing the Polaroids equally between us, once again with the promise to bring them to college with us. We kept our promises. After that, the mosquitos got too bad and we went back to our houses.

The last time I went to Benedictine was in July. I had been with my boyfriend, Mason, for eight months and I wanted to take him there because of how important the fields were to me. He liked to take pictures of the stars, so I told him to bring his camera. It was a cold night so I carried a stack of blankets. In cheesy high school fashion, I made a playlist of songs that reminded me of him and played them on my speaker. It was too cloudy to take pictures of the stars, so we bundled up in the blankets and talked instead. I was happy to be there with the boy that I loved and wished my first kiss had been here with him. Soon the bugs grew to be unbearable, so we folded the blankets and walked back down to the car. As we were packing up the car, a cop car pulled up behind us. I instantly got scared, knowing we weren't supposed to be there after dark, even if we weren't causing trouble. The headlights were so bright they hurt my eyes, and I felt like any movement I made was being scrutinized under a microscope. The officer came out and asked what we were doing there, to which we explained we had come to take pictures but were leaving because it was cloudy. The officer took our IDs to run in his system. I was panicking, though I knew we didn't have anything on our records for him to find. He came back saying we were good to go and reminded us not to come after dark. We drove off, my heart pounding.

I didn't know that Mason and I would break up in a matter of weeks or that that was the last time I would be at Benedictine before leaving for college. I wasn't afraid to leave Benedictine because it wasn't about leaving, but about coming back. I had left the Benedictine of my imagination the day I met the cop, but it was still a part of me. Growing doesn't mean leaving but building off of the person you were. From getting grass stains, to my first kiss, these fields were able to nurture the growth of my sense of self.

Note to the Reader

We hope you enjoyed our publication! If you have, we ask that you please consider writing a brief review for the book on Amazon.com. In your review, be sure to mention the title of the writing (or the name of the author) that you enjoyed the most—we will take reader reviews heavily into account when it comes time to decide who will receive our first solo-author book deals later this year!

About Z Publishing House

Begun as a blog in the fall of 2015, Z Publishing, LLC, has since transitioned into book publishing. This transition is in response to the problem plaguing the publishing world: For writers, finding new readers can be tremendously difficult, and for readers, finding new, talented authors with whom they identify is like finding a needle in a haystack. With Z Publishing, no longer will anyone will anyone have to go about this process alone. By producing anthologies of multiple authors rather than single-author volumes, Z Publishing hopes to harbor a community of readers and writers, bringing all sides of the industry closer together.

To sign up for the Z Publishing newsletter or to submit your own writing to a future anthology, visit www.zpublishinghouse.com. You can also follow the evolution of Z Publishing on the following platforms:

Facebook: www.facebook.com/zpublishing
Twitter: www.twitter.com/z_publishing

Author Biographies

Lauren Ashley: Lauren Ashley considers herself a "writer in progress." She has her BA in creative writing and English from Southern New Hampshire University and is close to completing her master's in the same program. She is still in the early stages of her writing career and hopes to succeed in her dreams of becoming a well-known published author. She is passionate about writing and creating characters that are complex and fun. She currently resides in Connecticut with her family.

Scott M. Baker: Scott M. Baker was born and raised in Massachusetts, spent twenty-three years working for the Central Intelligence Agency, and now lives outside of Concord, New Hampshire, as a full-time writer. He prefers the horror genre because it allows his imagination to run wild. Learn more about Scott at www.facebook.com/ScottMBakerAuthor.

Reggie Bourn: Reggie Bourn is a writer from New Hampshire whose work spans a variety of genres. While he prefers novellas, short stories help to fill the gap between larger projects. He is a rising sophomore in college, double majoring in writing and publishing/English. He can be found on Twitter @jcitsrb.

Jenell M. Boyd: Jenell is a lifelong resident of the New Hampshire seacoast. She's currently in nursing school and works as a nursing assistant in a hospital. When she needs to unwind, she enjoys writing, being outdoors, and traveling.

Kelly Dalke: Kelly lives near the New Hampshire seacoast with her daughter and husband. She teaches at GrubStreet, a Boston-based nonprofit writing center, Great Bay Community College, and occasionally at the University of New Hampshire. Her work has been published in *Flash Fiction Magazine* and *Litro*, and she is currently revising her first novel.

Jayson Robert Ducharme: Jayson Robert Ducharme was born and raised in New Hampshire. He attends Great Bay Community College and will transfer to the University of New Hampshire in the autumn of 2018. For five years he has been writing seriously and enjoys Southern Gothic, Modernist, and Russian literature. He lives in Salem with his Seal Point Himalayan, Dacre.

Stephanie Martin Glennon: Stephanie Martin Glennon is a Massachusetts attorney who writes a blog, *Love in the Spaces*, about her family.

Stacy Hannings: Stacy Hannings of Peterborough, New Hampshire, received a fine arts degree from Colby-Sawyer College in 2014. She is currently working her eighth season at an organic vegetable and flower farm and firmly believes baby animals are the cure to any bad day.

Niquie J: Niquie has been an avid reader since early childhood, loving how books created new worlds to escape to. She discovered the art of writing in middle school and has been passionate about it ever since. She considers herself an amateur Egyptologist, and she enjoys incorporating that rich history into her writing.

Kate Johnston: Kate Johnston writes adult and YA fiction and is published in *Compass Points, Wayfaring, Greensilk Journal,* and *Wolf Warriors*. She's a story coach, who inspires writers to raise their creativity to the next level. She loves to take nature hikes, watch Disney films, and bake ooey-gooey desserts. She blogs at www.katejohnstonauthor.com.

Elizabeth R. Jurgilewicz: Elizabeth R. Jurgilewicz is an anthropology and history major at Franklin Pierce University. Her work focuses on past personal experiences and their ramifications for the present.

James L. Kaiser: James L. Kaiser is from Derry, New Hampshire. Her second grade teacher gave her a journal to write in while she was waiting for her bus home after school one rainy day, and she has had an inextinguishable love for writing ever since.

Casey Kimball-Marfongelli: Casey Kimball-Marfongelli is a full-time student enrolled at the University of New Hampshire under the English program. He has had many experiences in writing since graduating high school in 2015. Having several of his works included in school newspapers, he aspires to publish more pieces in his future.

Leo T.F. Martin: Leo currently lives in southern New Hampshire with his extremely patient and supportive wife of fourteen years. He continues to write twisted historical fiction while looking to publish his first novel.

Kari Nguyen: Kari Nguyen reads, writes, edits, and raises a daughter and twin sons in New Hampshire, where she was also raised. She graduated first in her class from Colby-Sawyer College in 2004. Her writing has been published, nominated, awarded, recognized, and anthologized by some wonderful folks. Visit her at

Nolan R. O'Connell: Nolan O'Connell is a New England–based artist who focuses on subjects such as the nature and culture of the region. He primarily focuses on visual arts; however, he enjoys writing about his culture as well.

Carter Saltmarsh: Carter Saltmarsh grew up loving horses. As a child, he was bullied and tormented, and being called gay because he loved horses was a daily thing. But Carter ignored the bullying and because of a horse, he was able to stay strong and find the true human being he is today. He went off to study veterinary technology at Great Bay Community College and became a certified veterinary technician where he works with horses in an equine hospital, focusing on the health and treatment of horses.

Theresa Suarez: Theresa, known to some as Ree, loves to love people, loves to write, and loves to live life to the fullest. One of the ways she does that is through running, which she always has to give a reason for to people who question the sanity of people who choose to do things like that. But she's a psychology major with a double minor in literature in exercise science, so she knows enough about what makes someone insane, and she'd say . . . she definitely is! After all, a life taken too seriously is like not enjoying the toasted bagel with crème cheese that cost you over four dollars. So sit back with your bagel or snack of choice and enjoy some great works of art that *Emerging Writers* has to offer.

Nicole Turner: Nicole Turner is the author of *Benedictine and Me*, a memoir which takes place in her small hometown of Bedford, New Hampshire. She is now living in Boston, majoring in publishing at Emerson College. Naturally, she loves to read and write, but when she's not doing either of those, she's likely trying to travel the world.

G.R. Weslo: G.R. Weslo lives in New Hampshire with his dog. For him, writing is the only way he can get the crazy out of his head.

Marina White: Marina is an aspiring author and child psychologist. She is currently a student and works at a day care. She has her own blog, *The Kitchen Sink*, featuring just about everything!

Devin R. Wilkie: Devin R. Wilkie was born in 1989. He received his BA from Colby-Sawyer College, where he also served as a cofounder and editor for *Solidus*. He is a diversified linguaphile who has worked in education, bookselling, journalism, and book publishing. He currently resides in Lebanon, New Hampshire.

Made in the USA
Columbia, SC
11 February 2019